THIRD EDITION

FIELD PROJECTS IN ANTHROPOLOGY

A STUDENT HANDBOOK

JULIA G. CRANE

University of North Carolina, Chapel Hill

MICHAEL V. ANGROSINO

University of South Florida, Tampa

WAVELAND

PRESS, INC.

Long Grove, Illinois

For information about this book, contact:
Waveland Press, Inc.
4180 IL Route 83, Suite 101
Long Grove, IL 60047-9580
(847) 634-0081
info@waveland.com
www.waveland.com

10-digit ISBN 0-88133-685-8
13-digit ISBN 978-0-88133-685-6

Printed in the United States of America

19   18   17   16

Contents

Preface

Some of our undergraduate students have asked, "How can I know whether or not I really want to be an anthropologist if I can't practice being one?" How indeed? Practicing anthropology may include many experiences, but fieldwork, in particular, is often considered a sort of "rite of passage," a necessary prerequisite for one to be considered a bona fide anthropologist. We feel it can also be important for anyone who wants to understand basic concepts and get a feeling for the anthropological perspective.

Throughout a long period in the development of anthropology, students who were almost ready to go into the field for their first large-scale research learned from their major professors some of the ideas and techniques that had proved useful to them and others with whom they had worked. On at least some campuses, an aura of mystery seems to have surrounded this process of learning that would only take place at the feet of a guru. Even when some courses on field methods were finally created, most were tailored for advanced graduate students.

During this period only a handful of books gave any useful insights. Fortunately, anthropologists have begun to write insightfully and candidly about their fieldwork experiences in many ethnographies. It is this spate of new information that has been invaluable in the writing of this book.

Field Projects in Anthropology is primarily for undergraduates and for beginning graduate students. It is not intended as a complete manual of field techniques. Because anthropologists work in many kinds of situations, in societies that differ greatly from one another, they must be flexible, often learning in their own particular field situations a great deal about what avenues of approach to follow, what questions to ask, what projective tests to use, what kinds of photographs to take, what conversations to record — and also what areas to carefully avoid or delay in exploring. It would, therefore, be impossible to find agreement among anthropologists that *any* particular collection of projects, however chosen, satisfactorily represented the most basic and essential aspects of field research. Complete coverage is not our real aim. Rather, our aim is to present a series of projects that represent some of the most commonly used data-collection techniques. In carrying out the projects, each student will learn something about how and when to apply such techniques, or variants of them, in the field situation.

Students using the projects in this book under the supervision of their instructors will not merely pick up a few suggestions and specific facts about fieldwork techniques, but they will experience the special sense of excitement and personal satisfaction that comes from having established significant human relationships with others whose lifeways are different from their own, as well as having perceptively and carefully gleaned insights into their cultural perspectives.

The following fourteen projects represent areas of inquiry that have been traditional foci of anthropological research. For each topic we suggest a "method" or "data-collecting tool" by which the topic may profitably be investigated. This is to imply neither that the topic cannot be investigated by other means nor that the method cannot be used to investigate other topics. Moreover, it is obvious that no one research tool is self-sufficient. A good ethnography makes use of as many such tools as possible to gather a more nearly complete set of data about the culture being studied.

We believe that in the descriptions of the methods and in the selected bibliographies for each chapter we have left sufficient leeway for the student, working under the knowledgeable guidance of his or her instructor, to experiment, modify, or amplify the method to suit his or her own research needs. The selected bibliographies are composed of items that we have found useful in describing the topic area and in planning the project, but they are not in any way exhaustive compilations of all extant literature in any of the selected areas of study. The entries are mainly to be used as initial points of reference, and they are, for the most part, those works that are most readily available and most directly relevant to the suggested projects. The student, on his or her own initiative or under the direction of the instructor, is encouraged to go beyond these basic references insofar as time, energy, and research potential permit.

Although we present the projects in what seems to us to be a logical progression, we realize that the individual instructor must adapt the format of the book to his or her own particular course outline. In general, though, the following comments may be of use in planning course work.

The first four projects are designed so that even a beginning student in anthropology could reasonably carry them out. Each of them represents a basic area of field research and would be useful also as an early project in a more advanced field methods course. The beginning student can also get a feel for the "how-to" aspects of anthropology by trying his or her hand at these basic tasks.

Projects 5 through 9 are somewhat more complex in nature. They require periodic observations or other data-gathering sessions on the part of the student. Ideally, they should be started fairly early in the semester to give the student sufficient time to do full justice to the research.

Projects 10 through 14 can be made as complex or as basic as the instructor feels appropriate. Each can constitute a short-term effort, although more advanced students can make them the bases of more detailed, time-consuming studies. Project 14, in particular, may be used as a general summation of many methods and concepts in anthropology in the field.

It should be noted that some of the projects may profitably be done in tandem; for example, combining the photographic series (Project 13) with the observation of ritual (Project 5). We suggest that the instructor and student look over the project descriptions at the beginning of the course in order to be sure of ways in which efforts may be combined. Where it proves feasible, you may wish to carry out all or most of the projects with members of a single group.

Although anthropology is a serious scholarly discipline, we feel that it is also highly enjoyable. We hope that this book will help the student channel his or her natural curiosity about the customs and lifestyles of other peoples into anthropology's scientific framework.

Acknowledgments

Throughout the course of our writing, we have constantly solicited the comments and criticisms of our undergraduate and graduate students and of our colleagues. We acknowledge their help with deep appreciation, while claiming as our own the responsibility for any shortcomings in the book. Our research assistants for the first edition were Barbara Downey, Beverley Hurlbert, Linda Oldham Lester, and Isabel Terry. We again relied on Barbara Downey and Isabel Terry for the second and third editions, and also enjoyed the help of Dorle Kind, Donna Romeo, and Larry Metsch. Our patient friend Suphronia Jones-Cheek typed the third edition.

We are deeply indebted to those upon whose work we have drawn, some of whom not only gave permission for us to use their ideas but assisted us in doing so. They include Professors Donald L. Brockington of the University of North Carolina at Chapel Hill, J. Jerome Smith of the University of South Florida, and David M. Johnson and Gloria Wentowski of North Carolina Agricultural and Technical University.

For the third edition, three people each kindly read and commented upon one chapter in the area of their expertise: Professors Stephen Birdsall of the University of North Carolina at Chapel Hill, Malcolm Collier of San Francisco State University, and Richard Chalfen of Temple University.

We were fortunate indeed to work with Charles Mohler and Bonnie Monfort Bopp on the first edition and with Neil Rowe and Thomas Curtin of Waveland Press on the second and third editions. Their expertise and sensitivity in the realm of books were of great assistance.

Introduction

Anthropology is the science that studies peoples past and present, their cultures, and their life histories as groups. It is comparative, drawing material for analysis from a wide variety of societies around the world. These materials for analysis come originally from anthropological fieldwork — from archaeology and from ethnography, the subfield with which we are most concerned in this book. In the words of one text:

> The foundation of cultural anthropology is ethnography (Gr. *ethnos*, race, peoples and *graphein*, to write). Literally, the word "ethnography" means to write about peoples. As we use the term, it refers to the descriptive study of human societies. . . . Now, most ethnographic work is done by trained anthropologists who have carefully learned techniques calling for objective and penetrating observation and interviewing, empathic rapport, and accurate reporting. Modern cultural anthropologists are expected to undertake ethnographic fieldwork to become fully qualified anthropologists (Hoebel and Weaver 1979, pp. 12-13).

Thus, the research you will be doing in connection with the projects in this book is ethnography; and you will be acting as an ethnographer. The ethnographic material you produce in accordance with the project assignments will, however, constitute only a portion of the material included in a complete ethnography.

Anthropological fieldwork, unlike fieldwork in other social sciences, characteristically involves a long stay among the members of the society being studied in order for the ethnographer to get a more complete view of that society. The usual expectation for the person doing cross-cultural research in a region that has not been

1

systematically studied previously is that he or she will stay a year or more, so that the way of life of the people can be observed as it varies throughout the seasons of the year. The ethnographer must get to know a great deal about the total way of life before being able to understand selected portions of it. It does little good to be able to report that a group practices mother-in-law avoidance, parallel-cousin marriage, or any such custom if we cannot say why such a custom is practiced or how it fits in with other lifeways of the people. The anthropologist may find, for example, that legends and tales are an important part of the cultural history of a primitive people and regulate much of their social and political organization. Folktales and proverbs are often used as teaching devices for training young people in the society's value system. Songs, chants, honorary titles, and curing techniques are often considered private property, which means they are part of the study of economics. It is only when one approaches a culture as a consistent whole that valuable insights can be gained and the meaning and importance of any custom can become apparent.

The lengthy stay necessary for a well-rounded study of the lifeways of a people implies continual interaction with the group and better identification with them. The relationships formed between an ethnographer and the people among whom he or she works can, and frequently do, develop into lifelong friendships. Obviously, the ethnographer also becomes indebted to those who share their possessions, their time, and their knowledge.

The complete ethnography is the result of considerable fieldwork. It tells how members of a society live from the time they are born until they die, the positions they hold at different times in their lives, what they do in these positions and what the society prescribes that they should do, what the systems of belief current in the culture are, what kinds of choices in belief and behavior people have, in which ceremonies they may take part and in what ways, their art and bodily adornments, shelter, ways of making a living, and how this society is related to those nearby.

Getting to Know a Very Important Person: Yourself

Although the work you will be doing on the projects in this book will not result in a complete ethnography, you will learn from firsthand experience many of the things an ethnographer must know. You can gain this experience while benefitting from the advice and encouragement of an instructor and fellow students, do most of your research in the language you know best, never suffer through being refused a necessary visa, never find it necessary to write while in the throes of a virulent and exotic malady, never force yourself to smile bravely while consuming a succulent reindeer eyeball or a hundred-year-old egg that has been saved especially for you!

While these examples may seem a bit extreme, the fact is that an important part of getting ready to do fieldwork lies in coming to have a better understanding of yourself as a potential research "instrument." Perhaps, like us, you have thought about the anthropologists you know and come to feel that it is no accident that Professor A tends to work in a remote village or tiny island where he or she can know personally every member of the society while Professor B prefers urban anthropological research in a crowded city, Professor C works among a newly contacted primitive group in a jungle area, and Professor D studies the street corner society not far from his home. Few fieldwork projects are chosen solely on the basis of available funding or other practical considerations. Personal factors enter into choices—as indeed they should.

It is not too soon to start thinking about the factors that you would find important in choosing a future research locale. All anthropologists agree that the personal equation is of vital importance. The techniques of ethnographers are, as we have suggested, not so formalized that they can be used without consideration of who is doing the work. There must, eventually, be some consideration of the kinds of people you are drawn to, whether or not you can stand long stories of hunts or long ceremonial chants of ancestries, long reports of arguments or battles. Your interests are important too, and must play a role in your choices of research sites and subjects—perhaps as you carry out your research for projects in this course, but surely in any extensive research you plan for the future. We know ethnographers who are sufficiently motivated by their research interests and sufficiently unbothered by particular kinds of field conditions that they undertake by choice: research involving daily temperatures averaging 40 degrees below zero Fahrenheit; daily temperatures averaging over 110 degrees Fahrenheit, with no shade to be found; cycles of ceremonial activity that may allow little or no sleep for days on end; being repeatedly touched all over as part of becoming acquainted with some primitive peoples; having the hairs of their arms pulled continually while working among people who have never before seen hairy arms; and living in areas where water is so precious that the ethnographer must join "the great unwashed" for weeks or months at a time. Clearly, ethnographers who manage quite well under one or the other of these circumstances might do far less well under others—and so might you.

Other relevant personal factors are many and varied. They include, of course, the condition of your health, the health of anyone you might take with you, and the necessity to make adequate arrangements for medicine and emergency aid. Knowledge and ability in various local technical processes, games or music and art forms, or a lively interest in and talent for learning those skills, might also help to influence a choice of location.

So, too, might the fact of whether you travel alone or as a member of a group. Advantages of travelling with a family often include the increased ability to fit into a community and to be accepted with less suspicion, access to data on more age and sex groups in the community and, possibly, some division of labor. Advantages of travelling with a team include division of labor, cross-fertilization of ideas, some control of the personal equation, and access to more kinds of data and groups. Disadvantages of doing ethnographic work as a member of a group include the tendency to withdraw and interact too much with one's own group; the larger size of residence required, which may make one less accessible to the local people; the more drastic impact of the ethnographers' presence; and the greater drain on local food and other supplies. It is important to make every effort to avoid being a drain on scarce resources and, at the same time, to plan to buy or trade locally for as many things as possible rather than to import supplies. It is far better to make the effort to cooperate in these ways—in most cases, people will recognize and appreciate your efforts.

In general, getting to know yourself also includes developing a heightened consciousness of how best to draw upon your personal strengths—social, physical, mental—and how best to compensate for areas of less ability. (We all have them.)

As an ethnographer, the most important single aspect of knowing yourself lies in the ability to divorce yourself from the value judgments that grow out of the fact that you have been raised in a society that has a particular set of standards—moral, ethical, social, sanitary, and so on. *Ethnocentrism*, this business of being "centered" in, and seeing things in terms of, the culture of which one is a product (and that one may somehow think of as superior), is an anthropologist's main bugaboo, something he or she must continually and scrupulously guard against. For ethnocentrism one must try to substitute an attitude of *cultural relativism*, attempting to understand each trait in terms of the total culture. Occasionally, great harm is caused by well-meaning visitors to other societies who do not understand the local lifeways well. Examples include cases where native beers were discouraged or done away with and severe malnutrition resulted, where modern plows were sent in to replace wooden ones and the resulting compacted soils could later be moved only with dynamite, and where gifts of steel axes to replace stone ones resulted in a rather general breakdown of social relations. Even the experienced ethnographer can undergo culture shock when having to adapt to some kinds of living patterns, and every fieldworker must carefully consider the possible repercussions of his or her own actions.

We have mentioned that anthropologists are no longer merely the "sociologists for people with no clothes," and that modern ethnographers work in societies that range in complexity from little-contacted and technologically primitive groups to subsections of our own society. As you carry out the research projects suggested in this book, please bear in mind that you have a special challenge to perceive and to report clearly and insightfully upon the cultural patterns of people who are in many respects — especially outwardly — very much like you.

Notes and Queries on Anthropology states, "It is important that not even the slightest expression of amazement or disapproval should ever be displayed at the description of ridiculous, impossible or disgusting features in custom, cult, or legend" (Royal Anthropological Institute 1967, p. 32). At first some of our students greeted this statement itself with amusement and disapproval, but even after short research assignments near their own homes, they have often come to feel differently.

Some Ethical Considerations

Ever since the founding of the first anthropological organizations, there has been much attention to ethics. When the Society for Applied Anthropology was organized, for example, the preparation of its Statement on Ethics was a primary consideration. Some generally agreed upon ethical considerations for planning fieldwork follow.

The fieldworker must present honest statements about the research he or she is doing and how it will be used. This point cannot be stressed too strongly, for we have known people who placed not only their own research but that of others in grave danger by making false statements. People everywhere are accustomed to "sizing up" others. Since the ethnographer is constantly a part of the community, he or she will be under scrutiny as one who is interestingly different. Thus, any misrepresentation will very likely be found out.

Another major reason for sticking to true statements about the purposes of one's research is outside the realm of ethics; it is that the more completely and carefully one describes one's purposes to members of the local society, the better they can help with the research. The local people are the ethnographer's teachers about their society. They can make or break the research. We have both had the experience of finding that, once our purposes were explained, many local people turned into excellent amateur ethnographers, anxious to help us know their culture.

One thoroughly conscientious and kindly student of whom we know was interested in the elderly. She hated to state the purpose of her interviews to informants, feeling that, however she stated her purpose, it came out sounding depressingly like, "I want to interview you because you're getting old." She and her roommate decided it would be kindlier to say she was interviewing widows. As a matter of fact, for those women who loved and missed their husbands, it might actually have been harder to think of themselves as widows than as elderly persons. But the real point of using this illustration is that when the student wanted to continue her research on elderly women, no elderly single women, or married women whose husbands were still living, were referred to her because she had defined her interest as "widows." The jig was up when young Vietnam widows were brought to her and she could not use them in her project.

The nature and extent of the explanations one gives depend partly on the sophistication of the group and upon the nature and extent of the contact its members have had with outsiders. Anthropologists may start with an advantage in that people very much want their own anthropologist because nearby groups have had theirs. Or, perhaps, the people have a proud tradition of being kind to strangers and feel they can hear something new from them. On the other hand, one may have a great disadvantage in being mistaken for a government spy, a tax collector, or a "writer" in an area where writers have gotten bad reputations. It is important to find out what kinds of outsiders have bad reputations in order to avoid being taken for one of them.

One of the authors explained the purpose of her first field research by saying that she had been studying a subject that had to do with the different customs and habits of peoples around the world, and that her university had a requirement that, in addition to learning from books, each person should learn by living and doing research in another society. She had chosen their island because she had heard it was an interesting one to learn about and one about which people should know more. Didn't they agree? They did.

Others explain, for example, that the customs of different peoples vary greatly and that a study is being made of the peoples of the world. If told that the lifeways of nearby peoples have been recorded but that theirs are unknown to much of the rest of the world, most people will react favorably and want to add to the knowledge about their group. Telling about the customs of nearby peoples may, in fact, help in eliciting comments and comparisons. Some recent ethnographers have told their informants that the informants' own descendants would be likely to read their articles or books so this was a way to preserve knowledge for their offspring (Royal Anthropological Institute 1967, p. 33).

A second major kind of ethical consideration for the fieldworker is the responsibility for making clear as soon and as definitely as possible what he or she can and cannot do for the members of the group. You might need, for example, to make it clear that you are a student, working with very limited funds, and not the wealthy and indolent traveller you may appear to be, or that you cannot get jobs and entry permits for everyone who would like to migrate to your home country.

A third kind of ethical consideration lies in the area which recent United States publications call "Protection of the Individual as a Research Subject." This includes the ethnographer's duty to make and to honor promises of maintaining the anonymity of informants and to present the material as honestly and completely as possible, bearing in mind that the informants or their children and neighbors may read the ethnography someday. It also includes the idea that an ethnographer owes the hosts a great debt for their cooperation and must be careful to repay it in part by, for example, not reporting on them so that punitive agencies can take action against them. Maintaining the anonymity of informants includes not only cases where names must be "changed to protect the innocent," but also the responsibility for not using materials that could be traced to an informant by local people and used to his or her detriment.

In some cases where the ethnographer can easily be associated with a specific place, or an adequate description of the research locus and the culture would make it impossible to preserve the anonymity of the population or of people within it, other ethical arrangements may have to be made. For example, in a recent life-history project in a literate society, we found it necessary to tell our informants, from the beginning, that it would, for a variety of reasons, be impossible and undesirable to hide their identity. We told them — at the risk of losing "juicy tidbits" — that we would use their real names and perhaps even their photographs. When the life histories had been transcribed, each subject was asked to sign a statement that this was a true transcription of his or her own words and that he or she approved its publication with a group of life histories.

"Protection of the Individual as a Research Subject" includes many things and is an ongoing concern which should guide everything one does in the field. When you leave an area (and afterward when you have written about it), your relations with the people should be such that you would be welcome to return there and so would any other visiting scientist.

The final major ethical matter that we feel should be mentioned is the need to be sure of what a sponsoring agency expects from you when you accept its support, and to be sure that this does not include, for example, quasi-spy roles.

Before Going to the Field

An anthropologist goes to another society, or even to a different portion of his or her own national society, with a definite theoretical frame of reference, often one to which he or she has devoted years of formal study. Characteristically also, the area to which one goes is part of a region in which one has special training and with whose affairs one tries to keep up-to-date. It almost goes without saying that for any of your course projects that involve communities or groups with which you are not already quite familiar, it would be wise if you began as soon as possible to familiarize yourself with as many details as possible of the area where you want to work, and to meet some of the people whom you will want as future research subjects. You might want to begin by reading their newspapers and any existing chamber of commerce or tourism literature and by attending public performances and lectures, church socials, sporting events, and so on. Some members of communities close to university or college campuses may be weary of being research subjects. Hence special consideration and tact might be required in these areas.

Before leaving for the field and immediately after arrival, the ethnographer must be sure to secure permissions and clear any project with the proper government bureaus and officials. Visas for some areas take many months to secure, so their procurement may have to begin early. Some countries require, either as a supplement to a visa or as a precondition for its issuance, a certificate or letter from one's local police department, attesting to a lack of criminal status. Even where that is not specifically required, it may often be exceedingly useful. One of the things about which many governments or their officials like to be assured is that incoming people have sufficient funds and will not become public charges. It is often good to ask university officials to include such a pledge when they write letters of introduction on behalf of the ethnographer. While comparable arrangements in advance are, of course, not necessary for your projects in this course, please begin early to consider what arrangements you should make with officials and with the heads of any organizations with which you will be working.

Any equipment of foreign make that is to be taken into the field should be registered with local customs officials before departure in order to avoid having to pay duty on it when returning home. This registration can also be done in advance in many areas, which often saves time and avoids frantic rushing around when at an international airport or dock departing for overseas. It is also wise to check the customs regulations of the host country and be guided by their provisions. For a few countries, it would be wise to take to the field letters addressed to the local officials abroad from officials at a university or sponsoring agency attesting to the validity of the research to be undertaken and the legitimate need for the specific equipment and supplies. In your research for this course, although visas and regulations about importing goods through customs will be no problem, you might be well advised to check on what equipment and supplies you can and cannot "import." For example, many churches forbid the taking of flash photographs during weddings, baptisms, and other services.

The World Health Organization and other agencies provide useful information about health conditions around the world. Publications containing this information can often be obtained from a good travel agent or from the governmental agency where passports are procured. It would also be good to supplement this information with advice from anyone who has recently worked and lived nearby and knows the conditions of your field site. This applies not only to advice about shots and medicines to take along but to vitamins and diet supplements as well. For anyone who will be moving around a great deal or dealing with rough terrain (domestic or foreign), a tetanus shot is usually advisable, although tetanus boosters for those who have had initial inoculations are no longer given as frequently as they once were. These are all matters that should be talked over with a doctor during a prefieldwork checkup. Sometimes pharmaceutical companies will provide free samples of medication to scientists about to conduct field research. Occasionally, if the fieldwork locus has not been thoroughly explored for their purposes, a pharmaceutical company may give small grants to fieldworkers in exchange for soil samples or for properly prepared botanical specimens that will indicate to the company whether or not the site is of potential value for their research.

Checking transportation schedules and arrangements well in advance often pays, not only from the point of view of catching instead of missing the monthly steamer or the weekly plane or sloop, but because added familiarity with transport systems often results in better or less expensive service. For example, if arrangements are made in advance, it is sometimes possible to take with you on the same plane those things you planned to send as "air freight." By asking that they be taken "air freight" on the same plane, one may be able to avoid all the bother and expense involved with special pick-up and delivery and separate processing through customs, as well as the huge bill that would result if such things were carried with regular luggage and billed as "excess baggage." For the immediate purposes of your projects for this course, transportation may not be a major problem, but we mention it in order that you might include it on a future check list.

Getting to Know and Work with Others

We have written this book with the idea that "you, too, can do good fieldwork" as a general theme. We find that the aspect of fieldwork about which our students are most concerned (and we have been as well) is the matter of whether or not they can achieve and maintain rapport with the people among whom they work. As one anthropologist has put it, "The only information of value is that which people give freely. People do not speak freely unless they feel at home with the interviewer." Feeling at home with the interviewer is obviously related to his or her feeling at home with the people in question. Although the topics of beginning fieldwork and of interviewing an informant could form part of this introductory section, because of their importance we have made these topics the subjects of separate chapters. Please refer to Projects 1 and 4 for detailed discussion of these subjects.

Three Basic Principles to Follow

There are many rules that could be set up for fieldwork. You will find a good many suggestions throughout this book, but we have chosen to emphasize just three things we believe are of great importance. We urge you to keep them in mind as you carry out each project.

1. Label your work carefully. Each and every field note should be carefully labeled with the date on which the notation was made, a page number, and, if possible, a topic heading. A typewriter transcription of field notes taken at an earlier date should be labeled with both the date on which the notes were first taken and the date of transcription. Always make duplicate copies of any typewritten notes and store the copies separately for safekeeping.

2. Make extensive, detailed notes. This is an idea of potential usefulness in conjunction with your projects for this course, but will become vital for any extended fieldwork. We want to underscore it for several reasons. Presumably, most people who take courses in anthropological fieldwork methods do so because they are interested in their fellow humans. Such people may feel that they have been keen observers for a long while and have such excellent memories that they do not need to rely on extensive note taking. We urge you not to adopt this attitude. For one thing, a good collection of field notes can be of value for decades, and no one can remember perfectly all the myriad fine-grain details of a lengthy period of fieldwork and their exact time sequence. Secondly, an unexpected event in the future might make it essential to reexamine the happenings that led up to the event. Thirdly, an extensive collection of field materials can be mined again and again — now for details on one subject, now for details on another. Verbatim quotations or, failing that, close paraphrases of an informant's words, are especially valuable and help establish the proper tone. It is also an excellent idea to include in your field notes some indications of the conditions under which you were making the notes and — preferably in some special notational system that could not be read by the local people — thoughts such as "I have the feeling he is hiding something here," or "Remember to check this out with a specialist."

3. Check up on yourself. We have found checks of various kinds to be of value, both those in such compilations as *Notes and Queries, Outline of Cultural Materials, Field Guide to the Ethnological Study of Child Life,* and so on, and those that we ourselves have written in the field. Our suggestions throughout the book are merely starters. We hope you will use them as building blocks; but we suggest that, as often as possible, you

review your work each day, asking yourself what questions are suggested by the information you have recently uncovered, what avenues of approach you have not tried, which of the things you know perfectly well to ask and to do that you have let slip.

Selected Annotated Bibliography

Edgerton, Robert B. and L. L. Langness. *Methods and Styles in the Study of Culture*, 1974. Novato, CA: Chandler and Sharp. A favorite of ours, this is a simple and concise manual.

Hilger, Sr. M. Inez. *Field Guide to the Ethnological Study of Child Life*, 1966. New Haven, CT: Human Relations Area Files.

Hoebel, E. Adamson and Thomas Weaver. *Anthropology and The Human Experience*, 5th ed., 1979. New York: McGraw-Hill. One of the more popular general introductory texts.

Murdock, G.P., et al., eds. *Outline of Cultural Materials*, 5th rev. ed., 1982. New Haven, CT: Human Relations Area Files. A handy checklist for fieldwork.

Royal Anthropological Institute of Great Britain and Ireland. *Notes and Queries on Anthropology*, 6th ed., 1967. (revised and rewritten, 1971). London: Routledge and Kegan Paul. The best-known single anthropological field manual.

Spradley, James P. and David W. McCurdy. *The Cultural Experience: Ethnography in Complex Society*, 1988 (original 1972). Prospect Heights, IL: Waveland Press. Student-produced mini-ethnographies.

Beginning Fieldwork

One anthropologist began his book by asking, rather plaintively, "who ever reads introductions anyway?" We hope the answer is that you do, for the one in this book contains some information which may be of help in connection with the first project and many of your future research projects as well. As we suggested in that introduction, if you are typical of most of the people we have known who were contemplating their first anthropological fieldwork, you are especially concerned about the initial stages of your fieldwork and, in particular, about achieving rapport with those among whom you will work. Because these feelings are so common, one author entitles the initial chapter of her book on fieldwork "The First and Most Uncomfortable Stage," and speaks of beginning fieldwork as a stage where one lives in a social limbo, trying to behave as if one belongs and as if one knows what one is doing (Wax 1971, p. 19).

Since such a high proportion of all anthropologists think of their periods in the field as the most rewarding and exciting periods of their careers, despite having to undergo some initial discomfort, anyone seriously thinking of anthropology as a career should persevere in learning about fieldwork. Fortunately, students now have an opportunity to benefit from the experience of others, experience that is finally being written about more clearly and candidly, and in greater detail. Suggestions gleaned from the experience of many people are woven into each project in this book. Those in this chapter emphasize the initial phases of fieldwork.

Definite rules for making contact with members of other societies cannot be laid down. The attitudes of members of the host society will depend in large measure upon the contacts they have had with outsiders. Since, in some instances, those contacts have been very unfortunate, the ethnographer must take this into consideration and adjust his or her behavior accordingly.

Apart from the possibility of encountering extreme shyness or aggressive hostility, the ethnographer may be faced with any of a large range of attitudes requiring sensitivity, patience, and tact. In areas where other social scientists have worked and no benefits to the local people have resulted, the ethnographer may have to cope with extreme apathy and a feeling of superiority toward both the ethnographer and the items of material culture brought to the field. Local people who are smotheringly attentive because they want to exact favors or associate themselves with outsiders can be particularly embarrassing to the ethnographer who has not yet gotten established locally.

One general necessity upon arrival is to contact the local officials or leaders with whom the research has to be cleared. Presumably these are among the people with whom the ethnographer has already been in correspondence, if they are literate. The nature of the arrangements an ethnographer can make is often determined in large measure by the host group itself. The well-known British anthropologist E. E. Evans-Pritchard has remarked in connection with two of his fieldwork experiences in Africa that the two groups structured their relationships with him in completely different ways. The Azande would not allow him to live as one of them, but compelled him to live outside the village, and treated him as a superior. The Nuer, on the other hand, compelled him to live right among them and as an equal.

A first consideration upon arrival in the field is to establish a base of operations. Basically, for fieldwork of longer duration than any you will be carrying out for the projects in this course, this means a household. In other fieldwork situations, however, a vantage point in a sidewalk cafe, or some comparable locus, may become established as rather regular headquarters, either until permanent household arrangements have been made or as a supplement to them. You may also want to establish a part-time base of operations if you will be doing much of your research for this course in one area. Sites in the midst of the action of the community where observation is easier are ideal. Often the local people will be of help in this regard. Housing or research loci that are as much like the other housing of the community as possible will help to encourage the people to feel free to visit and, sometimes, to establish more relaxed neighborly relations in general. Maintaining a household in the field — especially where there is very little house to hold — can be very helpful in combating ethnocentric tendencies on the part of the ethnographer; especially where he or she is doing the housekeeping and dealing on a day-to-day basis with the many time-consuming and frustrating problems it can entail.

There are a great many aspects of establishing oneself in the field situation about which one can look to the local people for guidance. This may sound like such an obvious statement as to be unnecessary, but the fact is that many of us initially fail to profit from the clues that the local culture provides. As an example, we might cite the fact that in many areas "unattached" women who move freely about the community or live alone in guest houses are virtually unknown and may, therefore, be perceived as "loose" women or aberrant individuals. Female ethnographers do have some specific problems with which to deal, as most of them are acutely aware. We know one attractive female ethnographer who took her six-foot-three son along as "chaperone" on her second trip to a particular area. But six-foot sons are not standard operating equipment for most women, and the local culture may provide solutions. For example, in many societies it is the custom to have youngsters spend the evening and the night with those who would otherwise be alone. This custom can often be put into effect for the ethnographer very easily, sometimes to the obvious pleasure — even relief — of the local people, who are pleased to find ethnographers of either sex behaving in ways to which they are accustomed.

We suggested above that the ethnographer must, at least to some extent, accept and work within the social position the local people are willing to assign. On the other hand, he or she must proceed with considerable caution in establishing relationships when first in the field in order to avoid being associated in people's minds with undesirables. Unfortunately, sometimes those who make themselves most available do so because their fellow citizens find them less desirable. Nor should the ethnographer prejudice his or her reception by associating at first with a group considered pariahs by a group that is to be investigated later. For example, associating a great deal with untouchables and then trying to move to a very high-caste group would cause problems in India.

The preceding paragraph obviously suggests many potential problems. Some of these can be taken care of, or considerably lessened, by taking an important step previously discussed — carefully describing the purposes of one's work. We mentioned in the Introduction that this step helps people to understand and cooperate with the work. It can also help them to understand why the ethnographer wants and needs to work with all of the kinds of people who make up the society, not solely with the most prestigious, the cleanest, or those with the most education. Since getting to know people is not a one-way street, and the personal factors cannot all be controlled, the ethnographer can make his or her interests explicit and, in exchanging information with people, can let them know about his or her own background, family, and so on. With time and the establishment of understandings, local people may come to shield the ethnographer insightfully from those who would be potential nuisances. This assistance, however, is something to be watched very carefully lest problems be inadvertently created. A person supposedly acting on behalf of the ethnographer may unconsciously offend or unknowingly turn away people the ethnographer wants very much to see.

Every ethnographer in the field, however great his or her experience, is still very much the learner; the members of the host society, the teachers. Every culture has its own conventions, its rules of conduct and etiquette. These, and the common forms of greeting, should be learned as quickly as possible. In some areas where we have worked, for example, the common greeting is that of "doing your hand" (waving) to passersby. Those visitors who do it regularly are seen as friendly and interested in the local people. In order to be certain to do the things that please people and not blunder into doing things that are displeasing or offensive, it is best to make your desire to learn and your good intentions clear at the outset. It is likely that any unwitting mistakes will then be overlooked or regarded as ignorance on the part of a stranger.

In general, it is wise to move slowly at first. Care is needed because the areas that are sensitive topics for conversation may differ greatly from place to place. In some areas one must be guarded in discussing corruption, in others, avoid talking about physiology and prostitution, and in other places, be aware that secret cults or religious beliefs outside the formalized church are the sensitive topics. Learning the "touchy" points of a culture help one make good judgments about what questions to ask and when to ask them, when to take pictures and when to tape record. When Thomas Edison demonstrated the recording and playback abilities of his cylinder phonograph at a meeting of the National Academy of Sciences in 1878, women in the audience fainted. While few places in the world would produce such a reaction to recorders today, it is important to realize that your touchy areas may not be those of the local people. Perhaps public opinion will force you to move in where you would not have. When a death occurred for the first time in the community where one of us was studying, the ethnographer's first inclination was to observe the funeral procession and services quietly and inconspicuously, not intruding upon the family "in their hour of sorrow." Local people quickly let it be known that anyone with a camera should not be at the back of a crowd and urged, even pushed, ethnographer and camera to the most central (and conspicuous) place because, they said, obviously overseas relatives would like photographs of the deceased and of the large crowd that had turned out to honor her!

An interest in language, technical processes, music, art, crafts, or photography is not likely to be regarded with suspicion, and may often prove to be a better beginning for anthropological work than direct questioning. Someone who can take an interest in crafts or games, and can perhaps contribute something to them, will always have an advantage. A friend of ours who has the ability to turn his handkerchief into a fascinating jumping frog, a lazy turtle, or a hopping rabbit was quietly showing his creatures to a group of children in a Mexican mountain village when he found that they captivated young and old alike, and were wonderful "icebreakers." While you will be anxious to join people in their activities and perhaps to make contributions, you should not expect to have the new creations admired more than the local products. It is usually wise to assume the attitude of a learner, rather than that of a teacher, as often as possible, especially since that will consistently remind people that you are anxious to be taught.

In the first days in the field, while one is slowly becoming acquainted, anthropologists have found it good to begin with such things as mapping the community, assigning numbers to households and fields, and so on, so that ownership, working of the land, and membership in the household can later be made clear and explicit with number designations. General observations can also be begun, of course, starting with things like who goes to the well or standpipe with whom, who chats with whom, who visits whom, who goes to collect pension checks with whom, gestures, and identification of people within the group. It is also good to begin to become familiar with material objects such as clothing, houses, implements, and their construction patterns. Since the anthropologist in the field depends for so much information upon the things he or she sees, one must be observant and also able to organize and utilize observations. All such observations suggest topics for later questions and interviews and serve to verify interview data as well. In societies that possess the art of writing or of making other kinds of records, there may be scriptures; historical documents such as wills, deeds, or marriage records; inscriptions on stone, metal, or wood; and so on, that are sufficiently uncontroversial or public to be good subjects for early copying and study.

Much can, of course, be learned from early pure observation, but when tied in with participation and interviewing, observation becomes more valuable. In work with informants, the ethnographer uses two kinds of interviews, *nondirective* and *directive*. Nondirective interviewing involves asking the informant to discuss a general area of culture. Typical questions might be, "Please tell me about your life as a child," or "Please tell me more about _____." Nondirective interviews are used frequently in the early phases of research, since they allow informants to talk freely about things that interest them and seem important to them. This can help bring to light many things the anthropologist might overlook due to a lack of an equivalent situation in his or her own culture, and in giving him or her some insights into the perspective of the local people. The anthropologist must be willing to take into consideration all sorts of information of importance to the lives of the people, including that which contradicts pet theories or original formulations.

Nondirective questioning is useful throughout fieldwork; and, with the passage of time, more directive interviewing can be done. Directive interviewing means that the ethnographer, instead of suggesting broad areas for general coverage, asks more narrowly focused questions, zeroing in on specific things. (Being "directive," of course, does not involve implying answers to one's questions!)

In societies where questionnaires and standardized interviews can be used, the information they provide can be valuable for getting facts quickly, for checking on oneself, and, importantly, for getting information that is comparable from case to case. However, the ethnographer should frame and make use of questionnaires only after learning something about the culture and after a pretest. That is, before the questionnaire is administered, it should be tested by asking members of the local community to respond to the questions and/or to make sure that the wording and the concepts can be completely understood, and that the questions are relevant, fair, and inoffensive. It is also sometimes rewarding to find out what questions some local people would suggest adding to the questionnaire.

Whether as part of an unstructured interview or a questionnaire, the "hypothetical situation" can often be used to good advantage. The well-known scholar in African-American cultures Melville Herskovits was one of those who strongly advocated the technique for getting information about practices or traditions without referring to specific people or events. It is more diplomatic to ask, "What would happen if a boy were caught stealing apples?" than to say, "I understand your nephew was caught stealing fruit. What will happen to him?" Herskovits and others have shown that by using hypothetical situations, the ethnographer can free the informant to discuss happenings and patterns of events in ways he or she would not feel able to if talking about specific, real individuals.

As we have suggested, choices about which of the many kinds of questioning to use, the wording of questions, and when and of whom to ask them can usually all be handled best when the ethnographer has accumulated knowledge and experience of the culture. Characteristically, the fieldworker moves gradually from pure observation to more participant observation, from nondirective to more directive questions. When the ethnographer has established some of the kinds of relationships that will enable him or her to begin intensive fieldwork, he or she can move out gradually to other types of exploration. Rosalie Wax has described this stage in the development of a fieldworker so effectively that we can do no better than to quote her:

> Once the fieldworker has managed to establish some reciprocal relationships with his hosts, he will find, sometimes very suddenly, that his anxieties and his feelings of incompetence and stupidity have decreased to a marked degree and that he is able to work on a new and very encouraging level of competence. Indeed, the process of involvement is circular and cumulative. The less anxious a fieldworker is, the better he works, and as he becomes aware that he is doing good work, he becomes less anxious. Usually the essential factor in this transformation is the assistance and support — the reciprocal social response — given him by some of his hosts. It is in their company that he begins to do the kind of "participation and observation" that enables him to "understand" what is going on about him at his own speed and at his own level of competence. It is his hosts who will let him know when he behaves stupidly or offensively, and will reassure him when he thinks he has made some gross blunder. It is they who will help him meet the people who can assist him in his work, and it is they who will tell him when his life is in danger and when it is not. As this process continues, the fieldworker often becomes quite skillful and self-confident in his own right. He no longer lies awake at night tormenting himself over the question of whether or not he hurt this or that person's feelings or overlooked some particular opportunity. He finds himself doing with assurance many things over which, previously, he hesitated and worried for days. He learns how to behave in the presence of old people, young women, children, and infants. He begins to learn how to accept obligations and how to repay them, when to ask questions, and when to keep his mouth shut — in short, how to stay out of the most obvious kinds of trouble. Indeed, in the literal, ancient, and comforting sense of the phrase, he now begins "to know what he is doing" (1971, p. 20).

Between the lines of Dr. Wax's words, and in some of our own words, you have probably realized that someone who cannot abide feeling awkward or out of place, who feels crushed whenever he or she makes a mistake or when anyone laughs at ineptness, is bound to have a particularly hard time as a fieldworker. It is a basic fact that anyone conducting ethnographic research in a culture or subculture that is not one in which he or she was raised is a "ludicrous tenderfoot" who knows a lot less about what he or she is doing in some respects than a small native child, and that making fun of inept behavior has been a corrective measure through long periods of man's history. It is precisely because all of the people whose writings on fieldwork we mention in this book have had similar humbling experiences on the way to becoming more seasoned ethnographers that we all want to pass suggestions along, with a sense of sharing.

There is one thing that Dr. Wax stresses about which we too are willing to be rather hardnosed. She warns (p. 47) that "the most egregious error that a fieldworker can commit" is to assume he or she can win the immediate regard of a group by telling them that he or she wants to become one of them, or by implying that their tolerance of the ethnographer's presence means that the ethnographer is one of them. She points out that people seldom resent the person who wants to learn their ways or even to act as they do — imitation being the sincerest form of flattery — so long as the fieldworker makes it clear that he or she knows his or her role and that any newly acquired skills do not entitle him or her to privileges that they are not willing to offer. Nevertheless:

> What people do resent — sometimes very deeply — is the amateurish notion that the acquisition of a few tricks or a sentimental statement about universal brotherhood will, almost automatically, turn a clumsy and ignorant outsider into an experienced, hardened, expert, or sacred person like themselves (Wax, p. 49).

This does not mean that devotion to sentiments of brotherhood and high levels of motivation to work considerately and conscientiously are not appreciated by other anthropologists or by the people being studied. It does mean that the person will be judged much more on the basis of how he or she lives in a community and treats local people than upon anything said about intentions. Although the ethnographer may become the close and trusted friend of people in the community, he or she is different from them in various ways and will never completely become an insider, truly a part of the culture being studied. It is usually best if an ethnographer maintains his or her identity as a deeply interested, tolerant, respectful, and respectable member of another society. Emphatically, being a participant observer does not add up to "going native."

As you begin to contemplate the various projects for this course, please note that the first two projects will rely almost completely upon keen observation, and that the next two projects will each require you to work with only one informant. Thus, rapport building on a wider scale will not come until the later projects. Please concentrate at first, then, on striving to open "new" eyes on life around you. Perhaps you have spent your life thus far in a community very like those in which you will conduct your research for the course, or even in the very same community. There is a special challenge to working among people whom you have known rather well (or thought you did), and who may even be very like you in outward appearances. Whether or not you experience a mild form of what anthropologists call "culture shock" (the shock resulting from being confronted with an unfamiliar way of life whose clues may elude you), try to look at the situation as if you were a visiting foreigner—or even a man from Mars. Take nothing for granted; observe as sharply and objectively as you can. Try to develop the habit of being as aware as possible of what goes on around you at all times, and strive for new insights on old, familiar subjects as well as new ones.

Selected Annotated Bibliography

Anderson, Barbara G. *First Fieldwork*, 1990. Prospect Heights, IL: Waveland Press. One woman's witty and insightful account of "misadventures" during her first fieldwork.

Dumont, Jean-Paul. *The Headman and I: Ambiguity and Ambivalence in the Fieldworking Experience*, 1992 (original 1978). Prospect Heights, IL: Waveland Press. An innovative and insightful example of "reflexive" ethnography.

Fried, Morton H. *The Study of Anthropology*, 1972. Chico, CA: Crowell. A helpful book for any anthropology student, giving some attention to fieldwork, but also guidance and useful insights on many subjects.

Gmelch, George. "Caught in the Middle." *Natural History*, September, 1990:32-37. One man's lively account of problems that can occur when local people believe an incoming anthropologist is really from an unwanted agency.

Golde, Peggy, ed. *Women in the Field: Anthropological Experience*, 2nd ed., 1986. Berkeley: University of California Press. A wide-ranging collection of lively accounts.

Ward, Martha C. *Nest in the Wind: Adventures in Anthropology on a Tropical Island*, 1989. Prospect Heights, IL: Waveland Press, Inc. Ethnography showing the underlying realities of doing fieldwork on a tropical island.

Wax, Murray, Rosalie H. Wax and Robert V. Dumont, Jr. *Formal Education in an American Indian Community: Peer Society and the Failure of Minority Education*, 1989 (original 1964). Prospect Heights, IL: Waveland Press. Pioneering in its research methodology and its findings, this book helped to demonstrate the potential of ethnographic studies of schools and expose the deficiency of conventional testing research.

Wax, Rosalie H. *Doing Fieldwork: Warnings and Advice*, 1971. Chicago: University of Chicago Press. An engaging and helpful book that covers the author's own field experience and the lessons she learned.

Project One

Proxemics

There are, of course, a great many things that would make interesting research subjects for an initial excursion into "the field." We have chosen a topic that our students find challenging, and that has not been so extensively explored that you yourself may not chart some new waters. Our topic is *proxemics*.

We know that our spoken and written language is our most important medium of communication. We are also aware that we can communicate a good deal by the way we shrug our shoulders, stick out our tongues, or give dirty looks. But it is only in the last thirty years or so that Edward T. Hall and some of his associates have shown us clearly that "space speaks" and "time talks."

"Proxemics" is the term Hall uses in connection with man's perception and use of space — that is, he studies the relative proximity of people to one another in various situations and in various societies. He shows that how people handle space in connection with their human interactions can silently "speak volumes." Since each society of the world has different patterns of space use, we can distort intercultural communication easily and, by our use of space, give messages we do not intend. For example, the standard distances that people keep between them in public conversation in some societies — and it is important to realize that they are quite standardized distances — are far smaller than the distance observed in our society. When people from such societies come equally close to converse with Americans, they intrude upon the space we consider "personal," and we may unconsciously feel threatened and move away a little. The words of our diplomats may be carefully phrased, but, at the same time, we may be perceived as "ugly Americans" because of the messages we send by how we use space.

Like birds so evenly spaced on a telephone wire, each of us may, depending upon the situation, want an envelope of personal space around us. The size of that envelope depends very much upon the way that space use was patterned in the particular culture or subculture in which each of us was raised.

Hall points out (1955, p. 4) that in the United States "we have strong feelings about touching and being crowded; in a streetcar, bus or elevator we draw ourselves in. Toward a person who relaxes and lets himself come into full contact with others in a crowded place we usually feel reactions that could not be printed on this page." People tell children not to sit so close or breathe "down their necks." A male brought up in the northeastern United States stands eighteen to twenty inches away when talking face-to-face with a man he does not know very well; when talking to a woman under similar circumstances he adds four inches. A distance of only eight to thirteen inches between males, which Hall finds the only comfortable conversational distance in many parts of Latin America and the Middle East, would, in the United States, be considered either very aggressive or, perhaps, almost sexual. Hall portrays United States businessmen in Latin America as trying to maintain their preferred distances by barricading themselves behind tables, desks and typewriters, only to have visitors circle around or jump over the barriers in order to establish conversational distances that will be comfortable for them. Neither party is aware of just what is wrong when distance is not right, but both have feelings of discomfort and anxiety; both take offense without knowing why. On one occasion, Hall saw two men, one a Latin American and one a North American, begin a conversation at one end of a forty-foot hall and end it at the other. The North American backed the whole way down the hall trying to establish a comfortable distance between himself and the Latin American, who continually advanced, trying to establish his own comfortable distance.

To some extent each household establishes its own rules about privacy and intrusion; what may be a violation in one household in the United States might not be in another. Problems of intrusion within the home also arise from the arrangement and use of furniture. Many, perhaps most, families give each person a particular place in a particular chair at the dining table, and at meal after meal the family will follow the same pattern. If someone is allowed to sit in an absent member's chair, everyone realizes that it is only a temporary arrangement. Some widows recently reported that they felt sad to sit in their accustomed places, looking at the chairs where their husbands once sat, and they were happier when they moved to sit in their husbands' chairs themselves. Sometimes living room furniture is similarly regarded as off-limits to others. One of the authors recalls her family's embarrassment when, as a small child, she informed a prestigious visitor, "It's all right if you sit there now, but when my daddy comes home that's *his* chair." In a study of sailors in confined quarters, individuals gradually withdrew from one another or "cocooned," so that each respected the zone of personal space around the others. Where pairs were very incompatible in terms of dominance (both sailors either very high or very low so that they did not easily accommodate each other) there tended to be some contention over a particular bed, table or chair (Sommer, 1969, p. 13). Such "ownership" of places and furniture has often been reported in homes for the elderly and other institutional settings. In earlier times in the United States many churches required families to buy or rent their pews. This is no longer the case, of course; but many people still have a proprietary feeling about "their" pews. Several recent studies have shown that, especially in small churches, there is a strong tendency for people to sit in the same place week after week, and even occasionally to speak to an unwitting stranger who has taken the place and request that he or she move.

Numerous studies in the United States have shown the definite feelings people tend to have about their placement at tables. Working with discussion groups in a cafeteria setting, Sommer found that leaders tended to select the head positions at rectangular tables and others would arrange themselves so they could see the leader. Eye contact with the leader seemed more important than proximity. In a series of experimental jury sessions where the jury members filed into a room and took seats at a rectangular table with one chair at the head, one at the foot, and five on each side, there was a striking trend for one of the people seated in the head position to be elected foreman. People later reported that they felt selecting anyone else would have seemed like a rejection of the people in the head positions. It is interesting to note that the choice of seats was not random. People who were proprietors and managers chose head chairs, and in electing a foreman it appeared that jurors chose the person in a head chair who enjoyed the higher status. Subsequent ratings showed that people in the head chairs were believed to have contributed most to discussions (Sommer, 1969, p. 2).

Although the particular details of space use patterns differ greatly from country to country, studies tend to show that there is a fairly common difference between urban and suburban areas. In the city, where personal contact is usually limited to a certain number of acquaintances, the family and home are often closed to the outsider, although the larger society will be open. In sparsely populated areas the number of people one meets is small and the inclination to greet and know them is greater. Thus, in the United States, families who move to the city are troubled by the lack of overtures of friendship on the part of neighbors, and urbanites who move to the country are shocked when neighbors frequently drop in to gossip or borrow sugar. In Hong Kong, where more than three million people are crowded into twelve square miles, the Housing Authority manages low-cost apartments which provide approximately thirty-five square feet per person. When one of the construction supervisors was asked what would happen if the floor space per person was doubled, he replied, "With sixty square feet per person, the tenants would sublet!" (Sommer, 1969, p. 27).

How people use space can communicate in much the same way as tone of voice. It can be, like language, "formal or informal, warm or cold, public or private, masculine or feminine, and indicative of high or low status" (Hall, 1960, p. 45). Patterns of space use vary from nation to nation, and the same pattern can give very different messages in different parts of the world. Some findings by Robert Sommer suggest that space use differences may lie behind many recent difficulties in relationships between peoples of the Baltic region, especially Estonians, a "non-contact" people, and Russians, a "high-contact" people. One of our colleagues, a friendly fellow, was taken by surprise on a return visit to Russia last year when each of the men whom he had met at a conference on his previous trip rushed up, seized him in a Russian bear hug and kissed him on the lips. This is, however, in Russian society not at all unusual. In many parts of the world men embrace upon meeting or walk arm-in-arm. During Middle East crisis deliberations in 1990, when news magazines in the United States printed pictures of President Mubarak of Egypt and King Fahd of Saudi Arabia walking hand-in-hand, they felt they needed to explain it was a Middle Eastern custom.

People in every society grow up learning to move through space and interact with others in the patterned ways that their respective societies consider appropriate and that are related to the society's own lifestyle, patterns of architectural design, furniture placement, and so on. In Japan, for example, interior walls are movable and can be opened and closed as the day's activities or people's moods change. The walls screen visually, but, with only paper walls, the acoustic "screening" is minimal. Japanese tend to focus on arranging the furniture along permanent walls or in the center of a room, while in the United States we tend to arrange furniture around the walls, leaving the center of the room empty.

One thing that has been found to be generally true is that the vast majority of people in every society are not aware of how they are using space. In response to questions, they cannot say precisely why they feel uneasy or pressed in some situations, more comfortable in others. Obviously, we do not have to adjust our lives completely to conform to the space-use patterns of those with whom we are interacting. As Hall suggests, we are expected to be different, but we can learn to communicate better with others by being sensitive to the unwritten patterns to which they are accustomed. To be aware that there are pitfalls in cross-cultural relations on the basis of differences in space use is a big step forward.

Clashes between people who employ different systems of space use are not limited to international relations. Several social scientists, including Hall, report that while the members of many of the diverse groups that make up United States society may sound basically alike and look alike, beneath the surface there lie many unformulated differences in the structuring of time, space, and relationships (Hall, 1969, p. x). Commenting upon some of Hall's work, Weston La Barre (1968) makes some interesting suggestions regarding ways in which space use may be seen to differ regionally in the United States and to have a sex component, an age component and probably a status component as well.

The Project

The first assignment is to design and carry out an experiment in some aspect of how our society or some subsociety uses space. For example, you might focus upon how people use the tables in a library reading room. How is the use of tables and chairs different if the people know one another and/or come in together and converse at the table from cases where they appear not to know one another? Alternatively, you might want to examine how people arrange themselves on buses or trains, at clinics, or in waiting rooms. Please note that this may require more than one observation period, or a fairly long period in one place, to get the detailed notes you will require.

One thing you might find useful to explore is the extent to which the spaces you study and the furniture within them tend to keep people apart or to draw them together. Following studies by a physician named Osmond, Hall (1969, p. 108) speaks of such areas as railway waiting rooms as *sociofugal* (those that keep people apart) and some, like the tables at a French sidewalk cafe, as *sociopetal* (those that tend to bring people together). Sociofugal space is not necessarily bad, nor sociopetal space good, but an understanding of the concepts has led to insights into such matters as how to discourage crowding and clogging spaces that need to be kept free, how to encourage interaction between patients in nursing homes, and so on. Robert Sommer (cited in Hall 1963, p. 435), in a study on the effect of spatial arrangements on human interaction, rearranged the furniture in a model ward of a hospital where the patients had been apathetic despite bright and cheerful surroundings. "As a result of these rearrangements, the number of conversations doubled, and intake of information through reading tripled." Does your research suggest any ideas as to how changes in space use might bring about better human interaction or fewer misunderstandings?

This project in proxemics was chosen as the focus of a beginning chapter partly because it can be carried out purely on the basis of observation and can provide information of immediate practical value about space use, interaction patterns, and so on. Ideally, all of us should also consider these issues in an ongoing way, both in observing and understanding patterns of space use and in learning to be sensitive and responsive to such factors ourselves.

Selected Annotated Bibliography

Ashcraft, Norman and Albert T. Scheflen. *People Space: The Making and Breaking of Human Boundaries*, 1976. Garden City, NY: Doubleday. An interesting study by an anthropologist and a psychiatrist of some aspects of space use in United States society.

Davis, Lisa. "Where Do We Stand?" *In Health*. 1990, 5:34-36. A recent article which mentions a few new findings in proxemics.

Hall, Edward T., Jr. "The Anthropology of Manners." *Scientific American*, 1955, 4:84-90.

Hall, Edward T., Jr. *The Silent Language*, 1959. Garden City, NY: Doubleday.

Hall, Edward T., Jr. "The Language of Space." *Landscape: Magazine of Human Geography*, 1960, 1:41-45.

Hall, Edward T., Jr. "Proxemics: The Study of Man's Spatial Relations." In Iago Galdston, ed., *Man's Image in Medicine and Anthropology*, 1963. New York: International Universities Press.

Hall, Edward T., Jr. "Silent Assumptions in Social Communication." In David McK. Rioch and Edwin A. Weinstein, eds., *Disorders of Communication*, 1964. Proceedings of the Association for Research in Nervous and Mental Disease. 42 (December 7 and 8, 1962).

Hall, Edward T., Jr. "Proxemics." *Current Anthropology*, 1968, 9(2-3):83-95.

Hall, Edward T., Jr. *The Hidden Dimension*, 1969. Garden City, NY: Doubleday.

Hall, Edward T., Jr. and William Foote White. "International Communication: A Guide to Men of Action." *Human Organization*, 1960, 1:5-12. All of these references to Hall's work are results of his extensive research on how people use time and space. He has done more recent studies, but we cite these as our choices for especially productive ideas.

Sommer, Robert. *Personal Space: The Behavioral Basis of Design*, 1969. Englewood Cliffs, NJ: Prentice-Hall. A psychologist considers the effects of physical setting upon attitudes and behavior and provides a program for the creation of structures based on human needs.

Project Two

Making Maps

Mapping is essentially a way of organizing and setting down observations. The information recorded will be of importance throughout the research, and later can be used in connection with a variety of matters such as genealogical and census data. For the anthropologist, whether an ethnographer or an archaeologist, an important consideration behind map making will always be the ties between physical space and social relationships. The cartographic technique, in a sense, enables one to rise above the immediate range of vision and consider the features and relationships of larger areas, whether the view is obstructed by a natural jungle or a "concrete jungle."

As we noted in the first project, an activity characteristically beginning early in an anthropologist's fieldwork is "getting the lay of the land." The fieldworker constructs a village or regional map, showing housing, agricultural land, fishing or hunting territories, important water resources, and whatever else the project and research design make it important to know. If plots of land are owned or controlled by families, one can also begin to note such boundaries or divisions. If time is limited at first, it may be useful to approximate the relative locations of features on a sketch map, record a network of key distances between features, then refine the map later. Using graph paper may be helpful in early stages.

Map making is an excellent device for building rapport during the period when the reseacher is most likely to be uncomfortable in a new field situation. It can provide a readily understandable reason for establishing contacts with people. During their construction and later, maps help greatly by reminding informants and researchers alike of additional information that should be recorded. Please note that we suggested earlier that almost any topic can turn out to be a sensitive one in at least some parts of the world. Map making is no exception. Therefore, it is wise to find out about and benefit from the experience of others who have done mapping in the area. Here again, it is essential to inform people of the purposes of your work, so that you will be less likely to be thought a government spy or tax assessor.

Work with local people from the beginning of your mapping project, so as to benefit from their insights into what is useful and what is culturally significant in their area. Most people know their habitats intimately, especially if their livelihood depends directly on the land, which, of course, changes through the seasons. Rather than marking off an area with a superimposed grid system, or sticking strictly to the ideas given by government maps and data sheets, the fieldworker should be guided by local people in learning the culturally significant boundaries. Anthropologists in the Philippines and in the mountains of New Guinea find that the people themselves recognize far more types of soil and plants in their regions than are reported by formal survey. These "native categories" of soils and plants may also be significant in determining the location of fields and house plots. Many societies have concepts of land ownership and land usage that do not conform to the systems imposed by their governments. It is also a good idea to note local names for features of the landscape and to use them in eliciting data.

People everywhere choose units of measurement that have meaning in their daily lives, and all of these may provide clues for the researcher. A common request in our society is, "Let's get down to brass tacks," an expression that comes from the custom of driving tacks into a sales counter for use in measuring lengths of dry goods. Our admonition, "Mind your p's and q's" derives from the old tavernkeepers' warning to customers that they should be mindful of the number of pints and quarts already charged to their accounts. Harold Conklin has shown, for example, that among some Philippine peoples walking distances are stated in terms of the number of chews of betel nut one would consume on the way.

Cartographers sometimes speak of their art as a "universal language," practiced by people everywhere to at least some degree. Many fieldworkers personally experience the fact that the making of maps predates the art of writing in the societies they study. For the members of preliterate societies, knowledge of directions, distances, and landmarks can be a life-or-death matter. Devices constructed by some early Pacific islanders with frameworks of reed or midribs of palm leaves proved to be ingenious navigation charts for sailing between islands, each of which was represented by a shell attached to the frame. Eskimo wooden pocket pieces whittled in the shapes of portions of the Alaskan coastline have long been admired for their accuracy.

No one knows, of course, who made the very first map. The one that is believed to be the oldest in existence is a tiny clay tablet found by Harvard researchers in the ruined city of Ga Sur, 200 miles from the ancient city of Babylon. Like many maps through history, it was probably used to show landholding. Such landholding maps are called cadastral maps—their main use is for the purpose of assessing taxes. Although cadastral maps may exist for the area in which the anthropologist is working, they are one type of map that cannot ethically be accepted if officials expect in return genealogical or other private data that could be used to the detriment of informants.

Field Equipment and Techniques

The types and amount of measurement equipment the researcher takes into the field depend largely upon the purposes of the fieldwork, the climate, the nature of the terrain, and the nature of the maps and data obtainable from others. We suggest that a compass and a portable flat surface are important tools. If the proposed study focuses upon agriculture, for example, essential equipment may include rain gauges, a soil thermometer, and soil color charts. If the climate is tropical, corrosion-resistant implements, silica gel to remove excess moisture, and special tropical packs may be the order of the day. If fording streams or climbing steep, rough terrain presents special problems, light-weight equipment is necessary. An important step in planning equipment needs, therefore, is to seek the advice of those who have done similar research in nearby areas. Such checking might, for example, have spared past researchers the grief of having their too-beautiful rain gauges turn up as the personal adornment of informants.

Whether you have in mind the project outlined at the end of this chapter or some future research in "faraway places with strange-sounding names," there is one piece of valuable and complex measuring equipment always present: your own body. We suggested earlier that potential fieldworkers should get to know themselves as tools, and this suggestion applies to measurement. Measures of distance commonly used are the breadth or length of a finger, thumb, or specific joint; the span from the thumb to either the tip of the little finger or the tip of the index finger; the span from the top of the middle finger to the elbow (usually about eighteen inches—this is the unit called a cubit); the span over outstretched arms from fingertip to fingertip (the fathom); or various kinds of paces. Knowing the equivalents in inches for several of these units enables you to measure in the field even when you may be "travelling light" and have no other measuring devices available.

In sketch mapping, the main method for measuring distance is pacing. Surveyors or those who do a great deal of mapping learn to adjust their pace to equal one yard. While this method is convenient because it facilitates the conversion of figures from paces to yards and inches, it is not recommended for anthropological fieldwork because it takes considerable practice to maintain an even, one-yard pace when the researcher is tired and takes shorter steps, or when the terrain is very uneven.

The sketch mapper usually finds it desirable to use a natural pace and convert it to the equivalent number of inches or centimeters. The length of a person's natural walking pace is extraordinarily uniform, as may be tested by counting your paces along a street block or some measured course a number of times. It will vary somewhat if you are hurrying, if you are tired, if you are wearing high heels, if you are carrying heavy or bulky objects, or if the terrain is rough. As one cartographer has noted, "the human legs are quite an efficient measuring mechanism." However, as soon as one begins to count one's paces they become unnatural; practice is required to pace unconsciously. David Greenhood suggests, "The next time you are out walking, let the notion come over you to count every time your right foot comes down. Whether you are in town or in the country, just count, or grunt, or squeak every time your right foot comes down. Keep doing this until it becomes a habit, kind of mechanical" (1964). Counting only every second step reduces the counting but does not completely release the mind from concentration. If the distances to be paced are fairly long, you may want to use a pedometer, a small instrument that registers each forward step and shows the total distance covered on a dial.

An alternative to pacing that gives good results is measurement with the use of a wheel—a bicycle if one is available for your fieldwork. It is easy enough to find the factor of the bicycle wheel by riding it over a measured distance. Revolutions of the wheel can be counted by tying a little piece of cane or a springy twig to the front wheel so it will give a twang at each revolution as it passes the forks. The main problem with bicycle measurement is that it is much harder to cycle straight than to walk straight, so a margin for error must be allowed.

Another method is the time-honored one of "chaining," measuring a length by laying a cord, chain, or tape down successively along the survey line. This involves the assistance of a second person.

For some kinds of distance measurements, many researchers like to use pocket range finders which can be inexpensive and relatively accurate. As an alternative, use the range finder on your camera if that does not upset people or make them feel they are continually being photographed.

There are times when a good photograph may make an important contribution to a map, provided some requirements are met: the position of the camera must be known, and the camera must be held truly level. Include something that shows scale in your photographs. Vertical aerial photos, where available, are a great boon to the map maker. In recent years, landscape sketching, once a cherished art of geographers and some archaeologists, has fallen into disuse. Photography provides such quick means of obtaining pictures that few people carry sketchpads into the field. Field sketching has advantages over photography in some respects, however, in that it stimulates close observation, it makes possible the elimination of foreground obstruction, it facilitates the selection of significant features, and labels and explanations can be placed right on the picture.

Drawing the Map

If you are fortunate, you may be able to start with someone else's map. Copying, even tracing, is a common procedure in both military and civilian mapping, not because of laziness but to make use of good work that has already been done. Remember, however, there are copyright laws. Road maps, for example, usually bear a copyright; but, even in such cases, you may use the information the map provides if you do not use the maker's particular design, special symbols of his own invention, his interpretation and expression of detail, or copyrighted typeface designs. Note, however, that even some official maps may be inaccurate either as a result of original errors or because of changes that have occurred in the local landscape. Identify the source of any material that is not common knowledge or does not come from good public authority. In general, identification of source materials helps to establish the quality of your map. In most cases, when a cartographer working for the United States government makes a map, you may use it as a base map. In this country there are more than twenty federal offices publishing maps, among them the Geological Survey, Coast and

Geodetic Survey, General Land Office, and the Hydrographic Survey. Some, including the Hydrographic Survey, have maps of foreign as well as domestic areas. While planning foreign fieldwork, mention a desire to obtain maps in your contacts with embassy officials. In cases where army maps are involved, for example, negotiations may be on a government-to-government level.

Whether you are starting from scratch to create your own map or using the work of others, bear in mind the nature of your project and the related purposes of your map. The selection of important features and the playing down or elimination of nonessential ones is a vital part of map construction. Some ethnographers suggest that a fairly detailed map may be useful while gathering raw data because it reminds both informant and researcher of relationships in several realms. In general, however, uncluttered maps are best at later stages. Your first completed map will be a satisfying job, a lively expression of the facts of life in the community; but be sure not to attempt too much on a single map. Remember, too, that the maps produced by anthropologists in their published reports are intended as supplements to the reports, not as independent works.

Choosing the scale of the map you will produce is closely related to all of these matters because the scale sets limits on the amount of information that can be included and how it can be shown. All maps are reductions, but too small a size may overly limit the things you can represent. A map that is too large can be cumbersome, as anyone who has wrestled with maxi-maps in mini-autos knows. Again, you should be guided by the purpose of the map, making sure that the essential features can be handled adequately. Of course, in the field, portability is important. (It will also be important for your instructor when you complete Project 2!) An obvious alternative, when one has a wealth of detail to include but wants to avoid cluttering, might be to make two maps of the area, each showing a different category of information.

A cartographic draftsman who does freehand lettering; can use special pens, lettering sets, and all of the other necessary tools of the trade; and is knowledgeable about transfer patterns, papers, and so on, is rare—and, characteristically, very popular around anthropology departments. A lack of such manual skills and training, however, should not keep anyone from learning the principles of graphic expression. At some point, you may want to consult with or use the talents of someone skilled in drafting in postfield phases of your work. You may also want to call on a cartographer, especially if you plan to publish maps. A cartographer evaluates and rectifies data, and can make suggestions regarding the presentation of data based on modern theories concerning reactions to visual stimuli, and so on.

Since, in this book, we consider only simple sketch mapping of the type most ethnographers would expect to do in the field, there are no discussions of surveying or the expensive and complicated equipment it might entail. For more advanced information, particularly with regard to surveying, Spier (1970), Detweiler (1948), and the Boy Scouts of America (1976) are suggested. Two developments have revolutionized cartography in this century. One is remote sensing — the use of aerial photography, satellite imaging and radar. The other is the use of computers, which perform much detailed work that used to be done by hand. The National Geographic book mentioned in the bibliography gives a simple but fascinating discussion of these and other aspects of mapping you might enjoy reading about.

The Project

Construct a basic map or chart that you could later use in conducting a field study. You may chart a whole village or a segment of an urban or suburban area. It must be a real place with real people, and the assignment must take you into "the field." Please bear in mind that you want your map to be as useful as possible for investigating the lifeways and interaction of the people who live there. Include such items as railroads, roads and paths, bus depots, utilities, shops, the offices of doctors and lawyers, public clinics, police stations, firehouses, postal facilities, schools, churches, government offices, cemeteries, warehouses and factories. Your completed map should give anyone who consults it a good idea of the settlement patterns of those who live there and the placement of the human and physical resources available to them. Choice of the exact kinds of items to be placed on the map is largely left to you. Perusing the maps in some ethnographies may suggest categories you would like to consider. Note that the map or chart you are constructing may include areas that are markedly different in ethnic composition, degree of economic well-being, population density, household size, or other important variables of which an anthropologist should be aware in planning research. Any such important features should be treated in your map.

Please note that we have used the words "map" and "chart." Unless you are able to work with good aerial photographs or official maps as the basis of your project, it would be best to refer to the product you create originally as a chart, rather than a map, to indicate its lack of technical complexity. To accompany your chart or map, write a small statement to describe ways in which the area you have charted and its resources relate to places and people nearby. You might include information about changes that have taken place in the area, based on conversations and interviews with its residents.

The four maps included with this chapter were created for different purposes and in very different areas. Two are from sketches made by an anthropologist conducting ethnographic studies on a Pacific island at two different points in time (figures 2-1 and 2-2). Another, sketched by a student member of a team conducting an archaeological dig in a Mexican community, illustrates the context of the dig (figure 2-3). The fourth is the only one included that shows an anthropologist's use of published maps as a starting point (figure 2-4).

In the fourth example, an urban anthropologist working in the Middle East used a published map, but constantly checked and corrected it, constructing his own maps to show changes that had been made and cultural features missing from the cartographer's map. The anthropologist then asked several native residents to draw their own sketches of the community. Their maps gave the fieldworkers a far clearer idea of how people see their community and those features that they stress as important parts of their culture. It might be possible for you to pursue this idea, if you have the time. Talking with people about your project might also encourage them to mention features of which you are not aware or open some doors to you.

Although this urban map shows a whole city, it is not expected that those of you working in urban areas should attempt to map a whole city. The extent of the area within a city that you map might best be decided in consultation with your instructor, on the basis of the density of population and/or on the basis of being able to delineate and map one culturally distinct section within the city. In the absence of specific guidelines, eight square blocks in a city might prove a good area with which to work. Please note that a section of a city might not have all of the cultural features present within it that we suggested might be placed on your map. You might find it important then to indicate more fine-grain details. Bear in mind that you want to show those things that affect human relationships or channel how humans move within the area in question. It might then be relevant to show such things

Figure 2-1

Rough Plan of Taro Gardens in Rakisu, 1929

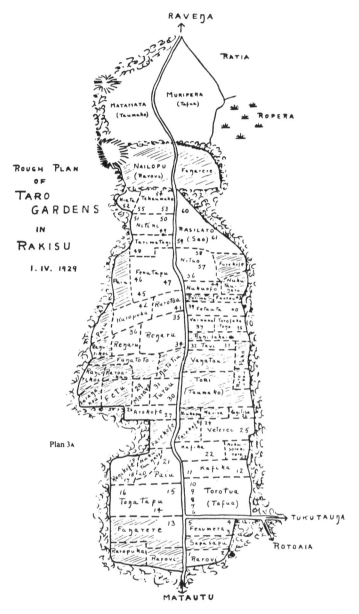

Source: From Raymond Firth, *Social Change in Tikopia*, by permission of the author and George Allen & Unwin, Ltd.

Figure 2-2

Gardens in Rakisu, 1952

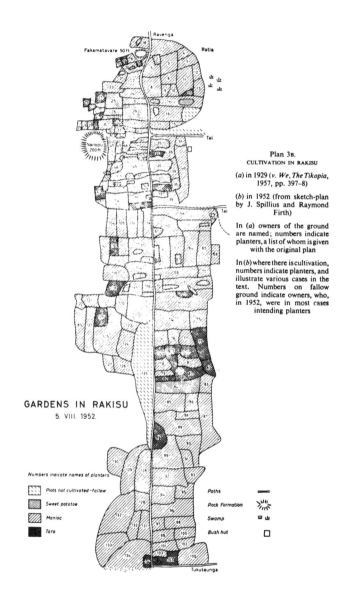

Plan 3B.
CULTIVATION IN RAKISU

(a) in 1929 (v. We, The Tikopia, 1957, pp. 397–8)

(b) in 1952 (from sketch-plan by J. Spillius and Raymond Firth)

In (a) owners of the ground are named; numbers indicate planters, a list of whom is given with the original plan

In (b) where there is cultivation, numbers indicate planters, and illustrate various cases in the text. Numbers on fallow ground indicate owners, who, in 1952, were in most cases intending planters

GARDENS IN RAKISU
5. VIII. 1952.

Numbers indicate names of planters

Plots not cultivated-fallow
Sweet potatoe
Manioc
Taro

Paths
Rock Formation
Swamp
Bush hut

Source: From Raymond Firth, *Social Change in Tikopia*, by permission of the author and George Allen & Unwin, Ltd.

39

Figure 2-3

Sketch Map of a Mexican Coastal Village

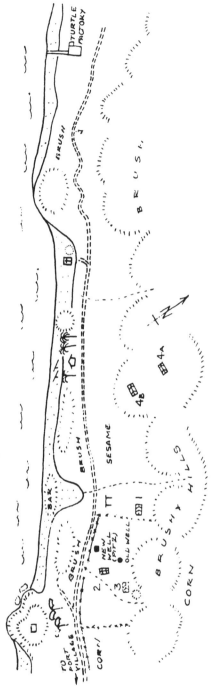

TT Shelter for corn

⊞ Shrine of the Cross

⊞ Houses: 1, Cervantes; 2, Ernesto's son;
3, Don Ernesto; 4A, Vasquez;
4B, Vasquez' son

⬠ American's house

⅄ Beach shelters

☐ Pumphouse for
Port Village water

🍌 Banana grove

🌴 Coconut plantation
(American owned)

⫶ Cockpit

Source: By Maria Jorrin. A graduate student's map of the community in which she was a member of a group conducting an archaeological dig.

40

Figure 2-4

Map of Tripoli, Lebanon, 1961

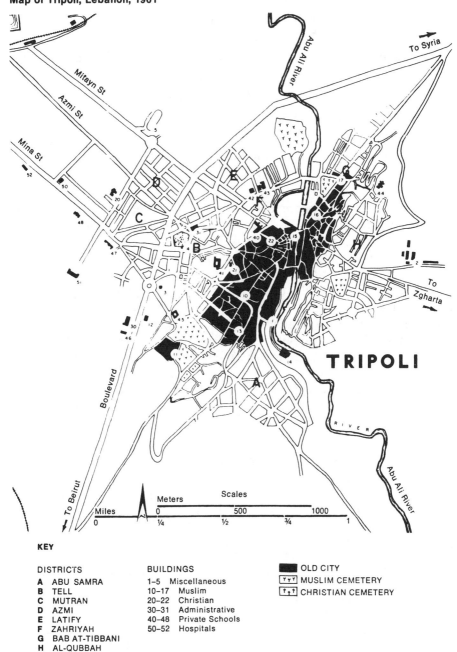

TRIPOLI

KEY

DISTRICTS	BUILDINGS
A ABU SAMRA	1–5 Miscellaneous
B TELL	10–17 Muslim
C MUTRAN	20–22 Christian
D AZMI	30–31 Administrative
E LATIFY	40–48 Private Schools
F ZAHRIYAH	50–52 Hospitals
G BAB AT-TIBBANI	
H AL-QUBBAH	

▪ OLD CITY
⊤⊤⊤ MUSLIM CEMETERY
⊤⊤⊤ CHRISTIAN CEMETERY

Source: From "Images of an Arab City" by John Gulick, pp. 179–197, *Journal of the American Institute of Planners*, August 1963, vol. 29, no. 3. Reprinted by permission of the Journal of the American Institute of Planners.

41

as bus stops, street lights, directional signs, direction of traffic flow, and police and fire call boxes.

Please remember the following four things that should be part of your map:

- orientation
- an indication of the scale used
- date of the map
- a key or legend

While a fancy "compass rose" design showing compass points is not necessary, there should be at least an arrow to indicate direction. Since every map is a reduction, an indication of the scale is an absolute necessity. Visual "bar scales" are favored over such statements as "one inch equals one mile," because when the map is reproduced a change in size will be reflected equally in the map and in the scale notation. It is as important to date your map as it is to date the other materials you create in the field, especially because almost all boundaries change from time to time, and it is difficult to search out the minor changes. Also, if you do future fieldwork in the same area and create a series of maps over time, you may have an indication of the rate of certain changes, as well as the direction of change. A good symbol is a conventional design that can be recognized without a legend. Such a symbol is either reminiscent of the feature it represents or has been established by long use in mapping. Even with good symbols, some kind of legend for at least a portion of the features of the map is usually necessary.

Selected Annotated Bibliography

Boy Scouts of America. *Surveying*, 1976. New Brunswick, NJ: Boy Scouts of America. Straightforward, clear, and very inexpensive.

Debenham, Frank. *Map Making*, 3rd ed., 1961. London: Blackie. A clear and thorough source, written by a British geographer.

Detweiler, A. Henry. *Manual of Archaeological Surveying*, 1948. New Haven, CT: American Schools of Oriental Research. Thorough but quite technical.

Greenhood, David. *Mapping*, 1964. Chicago: University of Chicago Press. A readily available paperback, often used in beginning courses in cartography.

Holmes, Lowell D. and Kim Schneider. *Anthropology: An Introduction*, 4th ed., 1987. Prospect Heights, IL: Waveland Press. A pleasantly written little text whose chapter on fieldwork in general and mapping in particular makes good reading.

Low, J. W. *Plane Table Mapping*, 1952. New York: Harper. A standard work on its topic — but probably more than you will require for some time.

Melbin, Murray. "Mapping Uses and Methods." In Richard N. Adams and Jack J. Preiss, eds., *Human Organization Research*, 1960. Homewood, IL: Dorsey. Contains some good suggestions, relevant for anthropology.

Monkhouse, F. J. and H. R. Wilkinson. *Maps and Diagrams, Their Compilation and Construction*, 3rd ed., 1978. London: Methuen. A standard reference on the subject.

Muehrcke, Phillip C. *Map Use: Reading, Analysis and Interpretation*, 2nd ed., 1986. Madison, WI: J. P. Publications. Does not deal with field mapping per se, but many different types of map construction are discussed.

National Geographic Society. *Exploring Your World: The Adventure of Geography*, 1989. Washington, DC: National Geographic Society. This fascinating and beautifully illustrated book is not one you need for the project in this chapter, but you might well enjoy and learn from it about mapping, measurement and many other things in your world.

Platt, Robert S. *Field Study in American Geography*. Chicago: University of Chicago Geography Research Paper No. 61, 1959. Covers field mapping techniques of many types and methods of field map portrayal.

Raisz, Erwin. *Principles of Cartography*, 1962. New York: McGraw-Hill. A classic by a geographer's geographer.

Ritchie, William, et al. *Surveying and Mapping for Field Scientists*, 1988. New York: John Wiley and Sons. A modern compilation with an archaeological emphasis.

Robinson, Arthur H. and Randall D. Sale. *Elements of Cartography*, 5th ed., 1984. New York: John Wiley and Sons. A good, solid reference.

Spier, Robert F. G. *Surveying and Mapping: A Manual of Simplified Techniques*. New York: Holt, Rinehart and Winston, 1970. Written for anthropologists, particularly archaeologists, by an expert — and an ingenious gadgeteer.

Project Three

Charting Kinship

Kinship is the topic anthropologists have studied more than any other. This is because, in the preliterate societies that anthropologists have traditionally studied, knowledge of the kinship system is crucial for understanding how each society is structured and how it functions economically, politically, ritually, and so on.

Anthropologists now conduct their research in societies at every level of sociocultural development from the most primitive to the most highly developed. While it is true that in some modern Western societies kinship ties are generally less important for large-scale organization, kinship remains an important aspect of social relations for every society in the world. As one anthropologist says:

> The family is man's most basic, most vital, and most influential institution. It is the foundation of society, the molder of character and personality, and the mentor of cultural values . . . . Family is what makes the difference between a "house" and a "home." It is in the family that man first learns to walk, to talk, and to function as a human being. It is where he learns the values that will influence his behavior all his life as he deals with the greater society. And it is where one acquires his self-image and his goals and his ideas of what he himself will someday seek in the way of a spouse and a home (Holmes 1971, p. 358).

It is the kinship system that determines the make-up of the family — in other words, how new members are recruited into the family (by birth, by adoption, by marriage, etc.), how the offspring are brought up, and how inheritance of property or position is regulated.

The ways in which people are assigned by their societies to various social groups are often quite different from the practices in the

Western societies with which most of us are familiar, and even from the ways suggested by objective biological facts. Consequently, this may be the first major item about which beginning anthropology students have difficulty in suspending their ethnocentric biases. For example, in many societies a person is not automatically assigned to the gender group for which we would consider him or her biologically determined. Among the Comanche and other warlike Plains tribes, those men to whom a warrior's career was repulsive were permitted to put on women's clothes and become accomplished at women's tasks. Nor is a person always assigned to an age grouping that has very much to do with the time that has elapsed since birth. The nature of kinship ties also varies from one society to another. A society may ignore or restrict natural "blood" ties or define them in ways that seem "unnatural" to us. It may artificially create a bond of kinship, or it may expand a natural bond to an indefinite extent.

The first important developments in the methodology of collecting kinship data and presenting them diagrammatically came from W.H.R. Rivers, whose "genealogical method" was first published in 1910. This method remains the foundation for most subsequent anthropological research on kinship systems. Rivers, like many researchers before and after him, found that most people enjoy talking about their relatives, past and present. Collecting genealogies, therefore, gives the fieldworker a convenient entry into a society and also provides important data about the basic structures on which the society is built.

Rivers used as few terms referring to kinship ties as possible in his first step, the collection of a person's "pedigree." He limited himself to using only terms for father, mother, child, husband, and wife. He began, for example, by asking his Solomon Island informant Kurka the names of his father and mother, making it clear that he wanted the names of the people who gave rise to Kurka's being, not anyone else who might be called by the same kinship terms. After learning that Kurka's father, Kulini, had had only one wife and his mother, Kusua, only one husband, he obtained the names of their children in order of age, and so on. He "found it convenient to record the names of males in capital letters and those of females in ordinary type" (1910, p. 2). Thus he constructed a chart, some of the features of which, as you will see, are still used in making genealogical charts. Kurka's chart looked in part as follows:

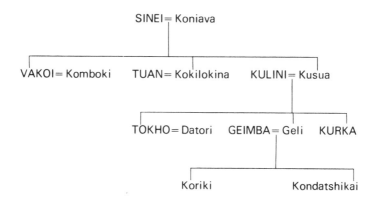

Rivers then used this chart with people's given names to collect Kurka's terms of reference for his relatives. Terms of reference are those used in speaking to someone about a third person, in the form "He is my _____." Of course, like modern anthropologists, Rivers collected such genealogies from many members of the community in order to get an overview of the whole kinship structure.

Charting Kinship Today

Modern anthropological kinship charts look different from those created by Rivers, although the basic principles and purposes of their construction remain the same. There are three basic kinds of relatives a person can have, all of whom may be found on his or her kinship chart. Consanguineal and affinal relatives can be found on every complete chart, and many include fictive kin as well. Anthropologists term the genetic connections between people *consanguineal* relationships. This means literally a "blood" relationship, although we are all aware that genes, not blood, transmit hereditary characteristics. Your consanguineal relatives, then, include your mother, father, grandmother, grandfather, son and daughter, uncles and aunts who are the brothers and sisters of your parents, and so on. *Affinal* relatives are those to whom relationship is traced through a marriage link. Your affinal relatives, then, include your spouse, in-laws, and the spouses of your parents' siblings. A large number of societies also recognize *fictive kin*. Fictive kin, simply stated, are those persons to whom ties are created where no consanguineal or affinal tie exists. The fiction may, however, have considerable importance and legal backing in a particular society. In our society the best example of fictive kin is an adopted child. *Ritual kin*, those linked by ceremonial ties, include godchildren, blood brothers, and so on, who are characteristically thought of as one type of fictive kin.

Diagrams of kinship ties are much more convenient and easily understood than verbal descriptions. It takes very little practice to understand and use diagrams. The symbols for male and female used by anthropologists are, for example, merely more convenient forms of the Mars [♂] and Venus [♀] symbols utilized by biologists and made familiar by the women's liberation movement. There are four basic components:

△ male

○ female

= affinal, or marriage, tie

| or — consanguineal tie

Note, then, that single lines are used to tie together all of the people who are genetically related to one another.

Difference in generation level is shown by running the single line down from parents to their offspring. Siblings (brothers and sisters) are placed along a single horizontal line from left to right in order of birth. Using the four components, the following diagram shows a family consisting of a father, mother, son, and daughter, the son being older than the daughter.

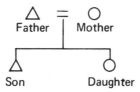

The family we have diagrammed is known as a *nuclear family*. The nuclear family, consisting of a pair of parents and their offspring, is a basic building block of kinship in almost all societies. Most people belong to two nuclear families during the course of their lives, the family in which one is raised as a child (the *nuclear family of orientation*), and the family one founds when one marries and has children of one's own (the *nuclear family of procreation*). To illustrate this for the daughter in the chart above, she might have two nuclear families as follows:

nuclear
family of
orientation

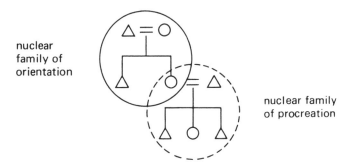

nuclear family
of procreation

The daughter's chart would be very confusing if we had not already suggested from whose viewpoint the chart was being constructed, and if we had not further clarified matters by circling and labeling the families. The people of the oldest generation might, for example, be thought of as grandfather and grandmother, as father and mother, or as father-in-law and mother-in-law by other people shown on the chart. To avoid such confusion you must draw every chart from the viewpoint of one, and only one, person. In every chart, then, show who is the point of entry, the person who is the central subject from whose viewpoint the chart is constructed (see example below). This person, called "Ego," is so labeled, or the symbol for the person is shaded, or both. Once we know who Ego is, we can correctly label the other symbols in the diagram. To save space and effort, it is common to use abbreviations that are simply the first two letters of the shortened word.

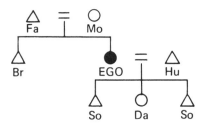

You may need other symbols for your charts, such as the following:

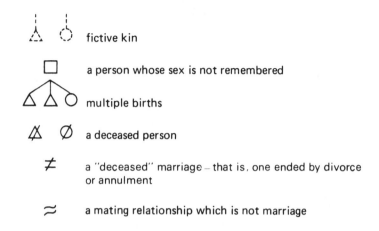

fictive kin

a person whose sex is not remembered

multiple births

a deceased person

a "deceased" marriage – that is, one ended by divorce or annulment

a mating relationship which is not marriage

For the sake of clarity, it may occasionally be necessary to move someone on the chart, while keeping his or her order of birth in the family clear. Two examples of such movements are included in the chart that follows:

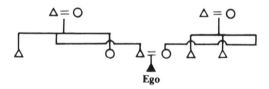

Ego

A chart for an imaginary individual is given on the following page to illustrate ways of using all of the symbols.

Note that, as in the case of Joe Doe on the chart, some people you are charting may have had more than one marriage or mating relationship. Be sure to show each pair of spouses with the equal sign between them, whether the unions took place serially or at the same time. To make your information clearer, it may be useful to number the spouses in the order of their unions to the person in question.

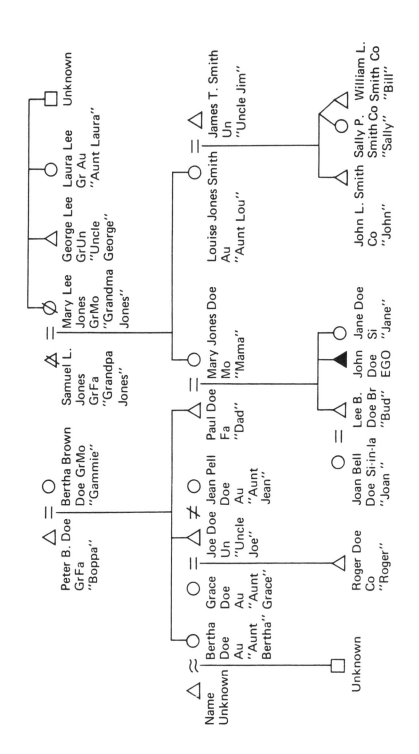

The Project

Interview someone and make as complete a genealogical chart for him or her as possible. If possible, work with an informant from another culture who can talk about his or her kinship in another language as well as in English, and who has a reasonably large number of relatives. Your informant will, of course, be "Ego" on your chart. Assign appropriate terms to each individual—the full name, the term of reference, such as "cousin" (the term your informant would use in referring to the relative while speaking with a third party), and the term he or she uses for address such as "Mom," "Slim," "Uncle Joe." (Terms of address are the terms one uses when speaking to the person in question.) For the sake of clarity, we suggest that you place the terms of address in quotation marks. If the informant did not know the person and therefore had no term of address for him or her, you may simply draw a line to indicate the lack of a term.

One kind of analysis that you can make even on the basis of a rather simple kinship chart is to test the common assumption that terms equating individuals reflect behavioral equivalences, and that terms differentiating individuals reflect behavioral differences.

In American English usage, for example, terms such as "uncle," "aunt," or "cousin" group together the relatives on both the mother's and father's sides of the family. The term "cousin" goes one step further and groups together male and female relatives. Ask your informant in what instances "lumping" people under a single term reflects social and behavioral equivalences toward such relatives. Also discuss how relatives have been recruited— by marriage, adoption, and so on—and the groups from which they came. Does your informant have fictive kin? If so, what is the nature of their ties to one another? If your informant's chart reveals patterns that are different from those you know well, you should follow the information and ask the questions that suggest themselves as most likely to lead to a clear explanation of what lies behind the terms collected.

Selected Annotated Bibliography

Please note that most of the references given below are mainly for the convenience of those who want to read somewhat more widely on the subject. Only the Schusky reference is suggested as particularly valuable for "chartsmanship" and the work of the project.

Bohannan, Paul and John Middleton, eds. *Kinship and Social Organization*, 1968. Garden City, NY: Natural History Press. A well-chosen and readable selection.

Graburn, Nelson, ed. *Readings in Kinship and Social Structure*, 1971. New York: Harper & Row. One of the many collections of basic articles on these topics. This one is mentioned particularly for the student who may wish to do more extensive reading on his own because it contains good introductions to sections that tie together the history of thought in this area.

Holmes, Lowell D., ed. *Readings in Anthropology*, 1971. New York: Ronald. One of the many good basic readers, this one is mentioned because of the material it includes on the family.

Holmes, Lowell D. and Kim Schneider. *Anthropology: An Introduction*, 4th ed., 1987. Prospect Heights, IL: Waveland Press. Mentioned here because this text has readable basic sections on kinship systems.

Murdock, George P. *Social Structure*, 1949. New York: Macmillan. A classic in the field, this book incorporates a statistical approach in comparing systems from worldwide samples.

Rivers, W. H. R. "The Genealogical Method of Anthropological Inquiry." *The Sociological Review*, 1910, 3:1-12. The article that started it all — referred to at length in the discussion of this project.

Schusky, Ernest L. *Manual for Kinship Analysis*, 2nd ed. 1983. Lanham, MD: University Press of America. Compact, concise, clear, readily available, and inexpensive, this is the single reference most used by anthropology students.

Project Four

Interviewing Informants

An anthropologist in the field wants to know as many people as possible in the community under study. If the group is reasonably small (a hunting and gathering band, a peasant village), the researcher can get to know many people as individuals. His or her descriptions of the community, therefore, will be based on repeated observations, and on the information gathered from a large number of these individuals.

Anyone who provides information for the fieldworker is called an "informant," but some informants are sought out because of their special knowledge. In the early days of anthropological fieldwork in the United States, for example, it was frequently impossible to meet and speak with all the members of a community because the community had ceased to exist. When it came to recording the cultures of almost-vanished Native American societies, for instance, the anthropologist often had to settle for the recollections of one or two old survivors of the group that used to be. In many cases these survivors were the only remaining sources of information about the cultures of departed peoples.

In other cases, anthropologists are unable to work with everyone, even if the communities they study are still intact. Limitations of time, money, equipment, and other research resources sometimes make it necessary for them to select one or two members of the group to interview in depth. An anthropologist then tries to select people who seem to have a knowledge of the ways of their group, and a sensitivity to the nuances of culture that is broader and deeper than that of their fellows.

There are other reasons why it is not always possible to become personally acquainted in depth with everyone who figures in a research project. The anthropologist might be working in a very large community, or doing a study involving the comparison of two or more communities. Even if it *is* possible to meet everyone and to cultivate numerous personal friendships, no one in a community will know everything about every aspect of the culture. Even in the "simplest" societies, there will be specialists or experts — perhaps a curer who knows a great deal about medicinal plants, an especially good hunter who knows animals and hunting techniques thoroughly, an old grandparent who knows the ancient tales or songs, and so forth. In these cases, the anthropologist can make the most efficient use of his or her time and energy by focusing questions on those who can give the most detailed information on their areas of expertise.

These chosen specialists will be the fieldworker's main links to the culture under study, although he or she must talk to and observe as many people as possible in order to get the full cultural context and the "flavor" of ordinary life in the community. One or more of these expert informants can be relied upon to provide the sort of detailed, specific information on crucial aspects of the culture that will be the core of the ethnographic report.

The use of a specialized informant generally involves some sort of training process. The anthropologist must instruct the informant as to the sort of information desired, and how it is to be recorded. This process has been especially true of linguistic fieldwork, where the informant must be taught to work with a fairly complex set of techniques and symbols. A short, on-the-spot course in anthropology is almost always required whenever the ethnographer works in depth with an informant. As a result, the fieldworker must be acutely aware of the potential bias in these situations. There is a danger that ethnographers, by telling informants what they need to know, and how that information is to be collected, may lead the informants to think in an unfamiliar way. An informant may end up telling an anthropologist only what the latter seems to want to hear, especially when the informant is an interpreter of language as well. Some degree of structuring is inevitable, but anthropologists must be continually on guard, and must at all times encourage informants to be spontaneous with their information. Informants should also be encouraged to volunteer suggestions as to what is and is not meaningful in that culture, and how those people tend to conceptualize and categorize.

In every human group, there are certain things that people "know" and that are relatively easy to conceptualize. For example, any of several adult men in a coastal or riverine New Guinea tribe would be able to tell an anthropologist how to build a canoe — if only because he could demonstrate the process in a concrete, step-by-step way. But every culture has, above and beyond its material creations, a set of values, attitudes and sentiments (see project 7) that are attached to those objects. For example, in his classic study of the Iatmul people of New Guinea, Bateson (1958) points out that the Naven ceremony, an elaborate and complex set of rituals, is held to celebrate a young person's first adult achievement. The building of the first canoe by a young man is cause for one of these great ritual observances. The building of the canoe has more than just a pragmatic value; it is a symbolic act related to the religious and kinship structures of the group. It would be easy enough to find someone to describe how to build the canoe, but it might be somewhat more difficult to find an informant able to express the deeper, more abstract concepts behind the physical production.

A number of anthropologists despair at the ambiguity of the concepts of "value," "attitude," and "symbol." As a result, some of them feel that it is futile to attempt to elicit such information from an informant. If we cannot communicate among ourselves what we mean by a "value," how can we possibly expect an informant from another culture to inform us about that group's values? An interesting study was done by Young and Young (1961) that statistically correlated the information they received from their key informants in a rural Mexican village with similar information gleaned from other sources (historical documents, folklore, projective tests). They discovered that while there was a high degree of agreement on the purely factual, concrete aspects of culture, there was very little agreement when it came to the more abstract aspects of life in the village.

Nevertheless, since anthropologists are perennially interested in what people think about as well as what they do, we must continue to ask questions about their values, even though we realize the possible ambiguities in that approach. We hope that impressions gleaned from one's informants will be supplemented by data gathered from the analysis of folklore or personal documents, or any of the several other techniques suggested in other projects in this book. No single approach to the collection of data in the field is foolproof. The anthropologist builds up a knowledge of a culture by asking the same questions in a variety of ways.

With this caution in mind, we may still be safe in saying that interviewing informants is a central part of the field experience. Anthropologists have long talked among themselves about the intensely personal relationships that they have developed with their informants. It is not surprising that an anthropologist, often isolated from familiar faces and activities while in the field, should respond so deeply to the one or two members of the community who most actively share in the research, and who are most closely involved in the day-to-day problems and projects of the study. Many an anthropologist has continued the relationship with informants long after leaving the field. Special informants are almost always rewarded by anthropologists. This reward may take the form of a cash salary, if that is appropriate in the particular culture, but it very often takes the form of an exchange of gifts or of other, more intangible favors (standing as a godparent for a child, bringing that child for education in North America or Europe, sharing photographs, contributing to the food supply in some way). Most anthropologists take the position that, since informants are giving up time and energy, they should be repaid in some way considered mutually appropriate and satisfactory.

The topic of relations with informants has come to be a distinct part of many contemporary ethnographies; Beattie's ethnography of Bunyoro (1960, 1965) and Chagnon's colorful portrait of the Yanomamö (1984) are two examples of ethnographies in which the anthropologists' informants stand out as individual characters in their own right, and in which significant parts of the books are devoted to discussions of relations with informants. Another interesting account of this kind is Powdermaker's warm and readable *Stranger and Friend* (1966), in which she discusses her fieldwork career and the several informants she has known and with whom she has worked. *In the Company of Man* (Casagrande 1960) is a collection in which twenty anthropologists pay tribute to their respective informants by recording their life histories.

Although working with an informant is so often critical to field research, it is not possible to walk into a village and immediately zero in on an informant. Selecting a good informant is, in its own way, a delicate art that most profitably grows out of the participant observation experience (see Project 5). As Pelto and Pelto have noted:

> . . . through participant-observation, the fieldworker notes which persons are most involved in the actions—they are usually the ones with the greatest amount of firsthand information. Furthermore, one learns about informants' particular "stakes" in social actions, so that one can assess the likelihood that any given informant might distort information to maintain self-respect or for other reasons (1978, p. 74).

Even after exercising the greatest care in selecting an informant, an anthropologist may still end up with a poor informant. Certain people in the group may push themselves forward because working with the "stranger" might enhance their prestige. Moreover, people who like to talk with the "stranger" are, as we mentioned earlier, frequently those who are shunned by their own group for one reason or another. The anthropologist Peter Wilson has written an amusing and informative account of his relationship with a local character who proclaimed himself Wilson's guide and protector, but who was, in the eyes of many in the community, a "madman."

Nevertheless, once one or more informants have been selected, and once the ethnographer is satisfied that their information is trustworthy, the process of "depth" interviewing can begin. The interview, as such, is a data-collection technique most commonly associated with psychology or sociology. In anthropology, an interview is never an isolated event, but is always a part of the participant observation process, an encounter with an individual whom one has observed in a variety of other contexts as well (Becker and Geer 1957). Nevertheless, there is much we can learn from interviewing tactics developed in the other disciplines because they have historically been important to anthropologists in the field as well.

Generally speaking, there are two types of interview: the *formal* and the *informal*. In doing fieldwork, the anthropologist often finds that some of the best interviews are the result of chance encounters. For example, one of the authors had the experience of conducting fieldwork in a monastery. The aim of the research was to have the monks recount the history of their community as it had grown and developed over the past several decades. One very old monk indicated his approval of the project but shyly declined to be interviewed because he thought it would be an act of personal vanity. One day the ethnographer chanced upon this monk, who was the community's head gardener, supervising the replanting of some bulbs. Stopping to inquire about the progress of the landscaping, the anthropologist was rewarded with a lengthy tale about a former abbot and his elaborate plans for the monastery's gardens, a chapter of the community's history no one else knew anything about. Since the ethnographer did not deliberately seek out the monk, and since he had no idea of conducting an interview (he merely asked the most general of polite questions), this was an informal interview. Most anthropologists freely admit that a surprisingly large part of their information—sometimes the best information—comes from such happy accidents.

On the other hand, some interviews will be more formal in nature, since informants are frequently sought out for their particular knowledge of special topics. In many cases, the subjects will be broached in a planned fashion, often at a precisely set time of day. Even so, there are two types of formal interview that the ethnographer may choose to have with an informant. The interview may be either *structured* or *unstructured*. The *structured* interview makes use of a prepared "interview schedule," a series of questions to which the anthropologist requires specific answers. The anthropologist should have some experience in the culture before trying to formulate such questions, since matters that may be "obvious" to people from one culture may be quite puzzling to those from a different background. Therefore, the interview schedule can most effectively be used as a summation device, used to pull loose ends together toward the end of the fieldwork period. A related type of structured interview involves the use of standardized questionnaires that enable the anthropologist to use a set of questions that have been validated in other research settings (or in the same culture, but at an earlier date). Its main intent is to collect comparative data, to see how these people compare with people elsewhere in the world, or to see how they themselves have changed over a period of time.

Unstructured interviews, on the other hand, allow the ethnographer to use the "happy accidents" of fieldwork to best advantage. For example, one of the authors conducted fieldwork on Trinidad, a Caribbean island one of whose main industries is sugar cane cultivation. He found an informant with voluminous knowledge of the sugar cane industry and set up an appointment to meet him in a canefield at dawn. Starting with the most general sort of question, such as "How is cane cultivated in this district?" the anthropologist was led by the specialist step-by-step through the day's activities. The techniques of planting, cultivating, harvesting, and milling were both explained and, if possible, demonstrated on the spot. The interview was formal to the extent that there was an announced topic and a planned meeting (for which the fieldworker was prepared with a notebook, tape recorder, camera, etc.). Some might claim that the interview was structured insofar as the anthropologist had to guide the discussion back to the topic when the informant digressed. But if the digression was very lengthy, or if it involved a subject of grave importance to the informant, the structured interview on the prearranged topic was delayed momentarily or even postponed.

The anthropologist's preoccupation with the given subject should not become an obsession. If informants are really concerned with personal problems, or if their attention has been captured by a new enthusiasm, they should be allowed to ramble. It might cost some time and patience and upset the fieldworker's timetable, but most anthropologists feel that rigid timetables are difficult to adhere to and that interesting information can often be gleaned from undirected discourse. Most importantly, the anthropologist realizes that in refusing to push the informant around in order to get back to the topic, good will is established; acting as a good friend who is willing to take the informant's feelings and interests into account enhances a sense of trust. If informants have been well selected for their knowledge of and interest in a certain topic, it is virtually assured that they will want to talk about it, in detail and at length, sooner rather than later, particularly since they will be pleased to be able to teach a foreign guest something of value.

In an unstructured interview, it is usually best to begin with the broadest, most open-ended questions, then fill in with specifics as one's own knowledge of the topic grows. Thus, one might start with an extremely broad question such as, "How is sugar grown around here?" This general query may yield a general response such as, "Well, we plant the cane when the wet season begins in June, harvest it at the beginning of the dry season in January, and then take it to the mill over the hill where it is processed and later sold, mainly as brown sugar or molasses." Vague and sketchy as this response is, it is full of information, and provides clues for more specific questions that are more likely to be intelligent now that there is some background to them. For example, "You say 'we' plant in June; who are the 'we' who plant? Do you plant seeds or shoots? Tell me how you do it." The informant replies, "In this district, the land is owned by the government sugar company and they hire only adults, both men and women. But the men and women work separately in the fields. Usually a new crop is cultivated from the part of the cane left in the ground from last year's harvest. We call this 'ratooning' the crop. The tips of the plants are stuck in the earth in rows, a few inches apart, and the area is cleared of all weeds. We use a steel machete and do this until the crop is ready to be harvested." This response may lead to even more specific questions: "Do the men and the women do different work?" "What do you do about the snakes and scorpions that hide in the weeds?" "Suppose the part left in the ground is no longer good — then do you start from seed?" In this way, all the details of the process are eventually brought to light.

Some anthropologists have found it helpful to use the camera to record someone doing something (planting a crop, making a wagon wheel, performing a ceremonial dance) in moment-to-moment detail. Then, once the excitement of the event itself is over, the informant can discuss and review everything that went on, using the photos as memory aids. Another useful means of approaching the interview is for the anthropologist to ask the informant, "Could you teach me how to weave a fishnet (make a stone axe, cook a curried goat, build a chicken coop)?" In this way, the anthropologist is not merely an inquisitive pest, but a friend who is willing to try to learn how to do something useful.

The first aim of interviewing an informant about some aspect of production, whatever means of approach are chosen, is to get at the mechanics of the process. Unless the anthropologist already knows a great deal about the culture, it is unwise, for example, to ask the canefield worker, "Why aren't you people in this district members of a union, like the people in that other village?" Such a politically charged question might be quite threatening to the informant. It is usually less threatening to start with the uncontroversial aspects of the craft—what materials are used, how they are worked, and so forth. Of course, there are no general rules about such things. It is conceivable that in some communities people will be eager to talk about controversial political subjects or other matters that might seem to be private or sensitive. Again, the anthropologist's prior exposure to the culture should be the guide in determining what is and is not a polite way to get a conversation rolling.

In any case, one of the main jobs of the anthropologist settling into a community and beginning to understand its ways of life is to find out:

- what people do in the culture under study
- how they do it
- what they think about the place of their product(s) or service(s) in the larger scheme of things.

The depth interview with the specialist is one means of getting at these three aspects of culture. Oddly enough, at the end of a field study, the anthropologist often has more specialized knowledge about more areas of the culture than any one person native to that culture who may be a specialist in only one area. In addition, learning how and why people do certain things and experiencing the frustrations of trying to do them oneself are fine cures for ethnocentrism.

The Project

Your project is to select a specialist who will agree to be your informant in showing you how to do a particular thing, and in discussing with you the social and cultural implications of that thing. Do not choose a skill or craft that requires a great deal of abstract explication. For example, do not ask a concert pianist to explain how to interpret a Chopin etude. Rather, choose someone with a craft that results in a concrete product. Interviewing an informant can, of course, be used to learn about a great many topics, abstract as well as concrete. But it is best to begin to hone your data-gathering skills with a topic that is relatively accessible. Find out, for example, how to make a leather belt, fashion a piece of jewelry, build a cabinet, plant a vegetable garden, build a model airplane, etc. Be sure that your informant is one who does this thing frequently, as a profession or an ongoing hobby, and who knows something about it beyond following the directions in a how-to manual.

Your report should be in two parts. The first should be a step-by-step description of how the product is fashioned, including a description of all materials and tools used. You may use a sequence of photos (see project 13) or sketches accompanied by explanatory captions. Whether or not you use photographs or drawings, be sure that your details are *specific and clear*, as if you were describing the customs of an exotic group to an audience that was almost completely unfamiliar with either the materials used or the finished product. It might therefore be a good idea to choose someone who creates a product with which you are personally unfamiliar, so you will be less apt to take details for granted. This exercise should sharpen your powers of observation and description, and also train you to ask increasingly precise questions about your subject.

The second part should be a somewhat more general discussion of what the informant does with the product and thinks its worth might be, then explore how the informant interacts with the people who buy or use it. Find out how your informant came to be interested in this activity in the first place. The precise nature of your questions will, of course, depend on the type of person you are interviewing, and on the type of work done. In general, however, you should attempt to find out the values and attitudes that are attached to this craft in the informant's community.

Selected Annotated Bibliography

Bateson, Gregory. *Naven*, 1958 (original 1936). Stanford, CA: Stanford University Press. A classic work in social anthropology, used in this chapter to illustrate the varieties of informant knowledge with regard to a particular culture.

Beattie, John. *Bunyoro: An African Kingdom*, 1960. New York: Holt, Rinehart and Winston. A good example of an ethnography in which the anthropologist makes explicit his informant relationships.

Beattie, John. *Understanding an African Kingdom: Bunyoro*, 1965. New York: Holt, Rinehart and Winston. A review of the methods used in the performance of one particular field study. Includes some interesting comments on the cultivation of informants.

Becker, Howard S. and Blanche Geer. "Participant Observation and Interviewing: A Comparison." *Human Organization*, 1957, 16:28-32. A comparison between the standard sociological and anthropological techniques of eliciting data from informants.

Bernard, H. Russell. *Research Methods in Cultural Anthropology*, 1988. Newbury Park, CA: Sage Publications. A recent survey text; see especially Chapters 9 and 10 on interviewing.

Bunzel, Ruth. *The Pueblo Potter: A Study of Creative Imagination in Primitive Art*, 1929. New York: Columbia University Press. A classic study of a craftsman's sociocultural environment.

Casagrande, Joseph B., ed. *In the Company of Man: Twenty Portraits of Anthropological Informants*, 1960. New York: Harper. Twenty anthropologists recount the life histories of their main informants.

Chagnon, Napoleon A. *Yanomamö: The Fierce People*, 1983. New York: Holt, Rinehart and Winston. A lively and readable ethnography with insight into how the anthropologist elicits information from informants under what may seem like extremely adverse field conditions.

Dean, John P. and William F. Whyte. "How Do You Know If the Informant Is Telling the Truth?" *Human Organization*, 1958, 17:34-38. A concise but insightful summary of behavior and attitudes that the fieldworker might well be aware of when interviewing.

Hyman, Herbert H., et al. *Interviewing in Social Research*, 1975. Chicago: University of Chicago Press. Geared mainly for formal interviewing (public opinion surveys), but note especially Appendix A, which discusses the selection of interviewers and includes case histories of particular interview situations. Note also Chapter VII on "Reduction and Control of Error."

Merton, Robert K., Marjorie Fiske and Patricia L. Kendall. *The Focused Interview: A Manual of Problems and Procedures*, 2nd ed., 1990. New York: The Free Press. Geared more toward sociology than anthropology, but with some helpful comments and suggestions.

Paul, Benjamin D. "Interview Techniques and Field Relationships." In A.L. Kroeber, ed., *Anthropology Today*, 1953. Chicago: University of Chicago Press. Although written from the general point of view of the ethnographer working in an exotic culture, this is still a valuable, concise summary of the participant observation context of interviewing, and one that is quite applicable to fieldwork in some segments of our own society.

Pelto, Pertti J. and Gretel H. Pelto. *Anthropological Research: The Structure of Inquiry*, 2nd ed., 1978. Cambridge, England: Cambridge University Press. A standard compendium of field methods and their theoretical foundations, noted here for the discussion of interviewing.

Powdermaker, Hortense. *Stranger and Friend*, 1966. New York: W.W. Norton. A warm and readable discussion of this anthropologist's career and of the several informants she has known and worked with.

Royal Anthropological Institute of Great Britain and Ireland. *Notes and Queries on Anthropology*, 6th ed., 1971. London: Routledge and Kegan Paul. A handy reference work; it is a categorization of questions to ask on the most commonly researched topics, and is thus a good checklist for interviews.

Wilson, Peter J. *Oscar: An Inquiry into the Nature of Sanity*, 1992 (original 1974). Prospect Heights, IL: Waveland Press. A valuable object lesson in how the anthropologist is not always in control of those who would be informants. Wilson ultimately made fine use of Oscar's "madness" as a means to understanding the dynamics of the culture of Oscar's community, but revelation was achieved only after a very bumpy journey with his self-proclaimed informant.

Young, Frank W. and Ruth C. Young. "Key Informant Reliability in Rural Mexican Villages." *Human Organization*, 1961, 20:141-148. An interesting study that statistically correlates information received from key informants in a Mexican village with information gleaned from other sources.

Project Five

Participant Observation

Field research is most typically conducted by anthropologists who are participant observers. They are not merely detached observers of the lives and activities of the people under study, but also participants in that round of activities. By becoming active members of the community, anthropologists need no longer be somewhat formidable "scientific" strangers, but can become trusted friends. By doing, insofar as it is feasible, whatever it is that the people are doing, they can have a first-hand experience in what such activity means to the people themselves. One's natural ethnocentrism is lessened as one is gradually immersed in the day-to-day circumstances of life.

Although participant observation has come to occupy a central place in almost all anthropological fieldwork, it is perhaps unfair to label it as a "technique" for field research, since such a term implies that there is one thing (or one set of related things) that a person does in order to *do* participant observation. In the last analysis, one does not *do* participation at all, at least not in the sense that one *does* a life history, or *does* a kinship chart, photographic series or opinion survey. Participant observation is more a state of mind, a framework for living in the field, than it is a specific program of action.

The ideal of anthropological fieldwork is the extended field study in which the researcher spends several months (or more) of uninterrupted residence in the community under study. Pioneering anthropologists in this century, like Bronislaw Malinowski and Margaret Mead, have been credited with "taking anthropology off the mission-house veranda"; that is, they went beyond the second-hand information gleaned from missionaries, traders, or colonial administrators and went out to live with the "natives" themselves. This accomplishment, however, represented the formalization of a tendency that had long been part and parcel of ethnographic practice.

In 1800, even before there was an "anthropology" in the modern sense, the French social philosopher Joseph-Marie Degérando published a brief, and almost completely forgotten, program for the study of other cultures. Degérando said:

> The main object, therefore, that should today occupy the attention and zeal of a truly philosophical traveller would be the careful gathering of all means that might assist him to penetrate the thought of the peoples among whom he would be situated, and to account for the order of their actions and relationships. . . . The first means to the proper knowledge of the Savages, is to become after a fashion like one of them . . . (1969, p. 70).

In one sense, the adoption of participant observation as the basic ethnographic strategy is a saga of the American frontier. In 1822, Henry Schoolcraft, a scholarly easterner, arrived in the frontier region of the upper Great Lakes to take up the position of Indian agent among the Chippewa (Ojibwa). His first helpful contact was with an Irish trader named Johnson, who had married an educated Chippewa woman. Schoolcraft soon became disenchanted with his "official interpreter," a besotted frontiersman with little understanding of, and absolutely no affection for, the Indians. When Schoolcraft later married into the bicultural Johnson family, he was able to get an inside view of Chippewa life. He began to understand that the errors and distortions about Indian cultures (from the "bloodthirsty savage" stereotypes of the frontiersmen to the "noble savage" romanticism of the European philosophers) were the result of constant trading in second-hand information. By living with the Chippewa, not merely looking at them from the outside, Schoolcraft learned that the Indian was "a man capable of feeling and affection, with a heart open to the wants and responsive to the ties of social life" (Hays, 1958, p. 5).

At one point, after spending some time living in the lodges of his Indian friends, Schoolcraft discovered that the Indians created myths, tales, and legends that they told both for amusement and instruction. Today we take it for granted that even the most technologically primitive people can possess an artistic tradition (be it graphic or verbal) of great richness and complexity, but it was a revelation of the first order in Schoolcraft's day. More importantly, it was a revelation that could never have come to him in his agency office. Discovering the "secrets" of the Indians required him to live among them as a friend who took part in their daily lives, participating in ordinary food-gathering forays as well as elaborate rituals, observing them from the vantage point of one who played as active a part as possible in their "real" lives.

In the Introduction to this book we discussed the problem of ethnocentrism that keeps people from being able to understand cultures other than their own. Even some of the greatest social thinkers of the nineteenth century were explicitly ethnocentric. Freud, for example, felt that Western civilization, for all its imperfections, was the pinnacle of human achievement. Other philosophers were willing to lump the "mind of primitive man" with the thought processes of children and/or people with mental defects.

Partly in reaction to these assumptions, anthropology in the twentieth century developed as an independent branch of learning. Confronted by the seemingly infinite diversity of cultures, and faced with the increasingly untenable nature of the proposition that Western people alone were "right," anthropologists formulated the concept known as *cultural relativism.* This concept implies that we must study all cultures with the understanding that they are adequate to meet the needs of the people who live by their rules. Cultural relativism makes it inappropriate to pass moral judgments about other cultures on the basis of what is deemed correct in one's own. If a culture were truly "inadequate," it would not enable its people to survive, and it would disappear. While it is undoubtedly true that Eskimo culture, for example, would be inadequate to prepare an individual for life in New York City, it is no less true that the culture within which a New Yorker lives in the city would be woefully inadequate to equip someone for survival in the Arctic.

Of course, people other than anthropologists have also appreciated the idea of cultural relativism when they lived outside their own societies. The Danish explorer Peter Freuchen, for example, lived among the Eskimo for many years. On the very first page of his *Book of the Eskimo* (1961), he states that the Eskimo possess a sort of "extraordinary hardiness" that enables them to survive in their harsh environment. But that hardiness was not strictly genetic, for Freuchen himself was able to survive in the same environment because he learned the appropriate elements of the Eskimo culture and used them to help himself adapt. Each culture must be understood as a vehicle for the adaptation of people to *their own particular circumstances.* The best way to reach an understanding of the "particular circumstances" of a people is to live with them. Direct experience with their way of life is also the most effective way to shed ethnocentric biases.

In the 1920s, Margaret Mead took issue with the then-common insistence that certain psychological factors, notably the "storm and stress" of adolescence, were universal, just because they were found in our own society. Mead was led to investigate the people of Samoa, a Pacific island which, in those days, was still relatively remote from outside influences. By going to live in the "native" village and by becoming an accepted member of a group of young Samoan girls, she was able to discover that adolescence in Samoa is marked by behavior very different from that which characterizes teenage individuals in the United States. In our society the burgeoning sexual feelings of teenagers are buried beneath social constraints. The Samoans, on the other hand, show a great deal of tolerance for certain kinds of sexual activity among adolescents. A major conclusion of Mead's research was that Samoan adolescents do not go through the period of emotional disturbance experienced by North American and Western European adolescents, who undergo psychological reactions to specific stresses built into their own cultures.

Considerable criticism has recently been leveled against some of Mead's conclusions, and against her purported bias in collecting data. But in her own time, the notion of cultural relativism illustrated by her findings in *Coming of Age in Samoa* (1928) and the later *Growing up in New Guinea* (1930) helped make the entire range of human behavior the legitimate subject matter of anthropology. This position gave anthropological researchers a strong reason to participate in the lives of people of other cultures, as well as merely to observe them.

The Project

Reading some of the classic ethnographies will give you a good sense of what it means to be an anthropologist in the field, but only by actually becoming a participant observer in some setting can one fully appreciate the implications of this attitude. It will, of course, be impossible for you to embark on a sustained residence in a community in order to do this project. But in order to get some of the feel of participant observation, this project will require you to spend some extra time in getting acquainted with an environment different from your own. You may, therefore, begin to be a participant observer in whatever group you select while you are doing other course work since the formal aspects of analysis and writing can be saved until the very end.

For the purpose of this project, you are to select some activity with which you are not personally familiar, such as the services of a religious group with which you are not affiliated. The remainder of this project will focus on aspects of participant observation that you might consider if you do choose a religious group. However, the principles translate into any participant observation project.

Religion is an important social and cultural feature in the lives of many people, and each religion tends to have its own particular practices, customs, personnel, and so on, making it a miniature cultural system in some ways. Moreover, most individuals are likely to have a number of unconscious ethnocentric judgments regarding religious belief and practice, so that it would be a real challenge for them to participate in the ceremonies of another religious community.

It is important to remember that you are not entering into the group's round of services merely to observe the rituals and chart the interactions — you are to be a participant in those activities as well, at least insofar as you are able to do so, given limitations on your time. This, therefore, cannot be a one-sitting project; it requires several visits, both to familiarize yourself with the rituals and personnel, and to make yourself known to members of the congregation. You may begin making visits to the religious meetings while you are carrying out one of the other projects. It would also be helpful (and more efficient) for you to cultivate the friendship of one or more ''key informants'' who are especially knowledgeable about the sect, and who are likely to extend your participation by inviting you to visit the homes of members of the congregation on a social basis. In this way, you will get a more rounded view of these people's lives than you would as an ''objective'' reporter sitting in the back of a meeting hall with your nose buried in a notebook.

The first problem involved in this project will be facing what we have earlier defined as ''culture shock.'' Even a trained anthropologist is apt to experience several kinds of shock (emotional as well as physical) in the first few days or weeks in the field. The anthropologist is, in a very real sense, an alien living in a social system whose cues have not yet been mastered. Of course, you will not be hit particularly hard by culture shock in doing this project since you will be involved in only one aspect of an ''alien'' culture, and since you will be living at your regular residence while you do it. Even so, do not be discouraged if you have a feeling of hopeless unfamiliarity at the beginning, a feeling that convinces you that there is something "wrong" going on in the service. Even so apparently trivial a matter as being confused as to whether one kneels, stands, or sits to pray can cause a certain degree of culture shock. The important thing is not to deny such ethnocentric feelings, but to accept them as natural and even to verbalize them, if you wish, to a sympathetic member of the congregation. Then you can begin to learn more about the sect, so that you can understand what is going on. Eventually, rituals that initially struck you as incomprehensible, ridiculous, or merely different will become meaningful to you.

It is not expected that you will come to embrace fully either the rituals or the doctrines of the group you are studying. Some anthropologists have had the experience of "going native" to such an extent that they experienced reverse culture shock when they finally got home. But no matter how much of a participant you become, you should never allow yourself to compromise your scientific objectivity. Moreover, becoming too much of a participant can become a severe burden on your time and energy. In line with this caution, it is necessary to point out that although many congregations are pleased and flattered to have an outsider express interest in their devotions, and will even welcome someone strolling in unannounced off the street, some with an aggressively proselytizing outlook might logically expect that anyone who is so interested in their services might easily be converted.

If you are therefore interested in studying a sect known for its zeal in attracting converts, it is only fair to speak to the minister or prominent members of the congregation beforehand to establish the fact that you are studying the group for a college course, and not necessarily for your own salvation. The leader or members should then have the right to decide whether or not you will continue to be welcome. Although sects that are not necessarily geared to conversion or revival probably require no such formal statement of purpose at the outset, you may feel more comfortable (that is, less sneaky) if you announce your intentions at the beginning, if only to one or two key members of the group. If, however, you want to work with groups that depend, to one degree or another, on "secret" ceremonies, or that indulge in activities that may go beyond what is strictly approved by the law (for example, snake-handling cults), you would certainly be well advised to explain your purposes thoroughly to the leaders and then seek permission from the group before embarking on your study. In certain exotic societies, the role of "student" would be meaningless, and the anthropologist would have to find some alternate term of explanation. But in most cases in our society, the role of student is sufficiently clear and, for the most part, readily accepted.

In all cases, your entry into the congregation will be considerably eased if you make the prior acquaintance of a member of the sect who could then be your initial guide, introducing you to fellow members and reassuring them about your motives. Needless to say, your informant should be an individual who is respected and trusted by the others, if it is possible to perceive who such members are. Remember that, regardless of your own feelings about religion in general, or about this sect in particular, religion is taken very seriously by many people. Your behavior should never be the cause for the disruption of any service, or for arousing controversy among the members of the congregation.

Two sociologists, von Hoffman and Cassidy (1956-57), have described their experience in studying a Pentecostal church congregation in a large city. They decided to approach the church first by playing what they thought was the anthropological game of participant observation, and they passed themselves off as potential converts. But they began to feel that this role was hampering them, because they were far too concerned with role playing and defining their own place within the congregation. As they found out later on, the members of the group were by no means as concerned with them as they were with the members, and everyone was relieved when the two dropped their poses and admitted to being researchers who were happy to be part of the activity but were not integral parts of the congregation. They ruefully recalled that "participant observation has been described as the business of being a professional fifth wheel" (p. 195).

Although the other research tools described in this book will help you to build up the information needed to describe and analyze a situation, it is participant observation that will allow you to do ultimate justice to both the description and the analysis. The data elicited by formal surveys of whatever type are flat unless they are underscored by the perceptions of a trained and *sensitive* observer. And no analysis, no matter how statistically elegant, can be meaningful in human terms unless it has been filtered through the deeper layers of meaning that only one who has taken part in that community's activities can possess. No one can ever know a culture as well as someone who was born into it and who lives with it on a day-to-day basis. Yet most "natives" are unable to discuss and interpret their own behavior because they take so much of it for granted. Insofar as anthropology can make a special contribution to the study of human behavior, it does so because the fieldworker combines the perceptive faculties of a trained, objective observer with the personal insight of someone who has lived as a member of the group over a long period. Neither aspect should be allowed to dominate the other.

In doing this project, you will doubtless be an observer long before you feel yourself to be a real participant. Therefore, at the outset, concentrate on being an observer. Some of the aspects you might want to observe as closely as possible and try to describe as clearly as possible include:

• The physical layout of the service: where is it held? how is the room arranged? what furniture or other paraphernalia are present?

• The human dimension: how many people are attending? relative numbers of men and women, adults and children? physical characteristics of the participants? interactions among participants?

• Aspects of ceremonialism: time of day? specialized personnel? special objects?

• The ceremony itself: who does what? when? what objects are used? how do people express their participation?

You may, if you wish, consult an encyclopedia of religion or other sources on the group you are studying in order to help yourself become oriented to the nature of the service and some of the beliefs that stand behind it. But try, at this stage, to keep your observations as "pure" as possible. Try to develop your own powers of careful observation and learn to rely on them. They are the only tools that an ethnographer is always sure to have handy in the field.

After you are accepted by the congregation, and as you meet individuals whom you particularly trust as key informants, you can begin to learn from the latter:

• how they became members
• why they became members
• how often they participate
• whether they participate with family, friends, or alone

You might also get these key informants to tell you what the ceremonies are all about. You need not be concerned yet with whether their descriptions agree with yours, or whether the descriptions of ordinary members agree with those of the leaders.

At this point, merely record information as given, taking note of discrepancies to be checked at a later date.

Finally, as a result of your participation in the services, you will get to know the activities fairly well, and will be well established with many members of the congregation. Now you can begin to check the discrepancies of description. Were there things you perceived incorrectly at first because of your lack of experience? Or had the members, due to their deep involvement, misconceived some aspect of the services that was more apparent to you, coming from the outside?

Your report should be a summary of your answers to these questions. You may also suggest some reasons why aspects of the service that might at first seem unusual or illogical are actually logically linked to the beliefs of the people.

One additional factor to be aware of when reporting your data is the potential bias arising out of participation itself. The very presence of an outsider — no matter how friendly and how much a part of the group he or she may be — means that certain actions and reactions among the members of the congregation may be changed or modified. In drawing up your descriptions, try to sort out any aspects of behavior that might be the result of this type of biased behavior. Such modifications, of course, will be more frequent at the beginning of the study, when you are still something of a novelty.

Students who have access to large communities might wish to use this project to experiment a bit with the nature of participant observation data. To do so, first select a sect that has several local congregations, such as several parishes of the Roman Catholic church in different parts of a city. Each student in the class will take one of these parishes to study in the manner suggested above. At the end, the students will meet to compare the data collected from all the studies to determine if there are any significant differences. If there is a disparity in the descriptions presented, you might find it very useful to attempt to learn the reason for such different conclusions. They may be attributable to one or more of the following:

- differences among the local congregations
- differences in outlook among the various observers
- differences among the observers in *method* of observation (that is, total time devoted to observation, whether one's chief informants are mostly men or mostly women, and so on)

If there does seem to be a significant difference among observers, try to set down the precise areas of disagreement. Those students whose conclusions differ might then visit the congregations where others received contrasting impressions and wrote different conclusions. There is, of course, no need to force agreement among all the students on all aspects of the study. It is, however, often helpful to compare research results because you can then better understand yourself as a fieldworker. It might be useful to hold a panel discussion on your several reports.

Selected Annotated Bibliography

Bowen, Elenore Smith (Laura Bohannan). *Return to Laughter*, 1954. New York: Harper. The original version of a novel by a noted anthropologist, writing under a pen name, which describes the personal, ethical, and emotional adjustments of one participant observer in the field.

Degérando, Joseph-Marie. *The Observation of Savage Peoples*, translated by F.C.T. Moore, 1969. Berkeley: University of California Press. The recently resurrected program for a participant observation approach to social anthropology. Despite the quaintness of language, Degérando's insights are startlingly contemporary and still very relevant.

Freuchen, Peter. *Book of the Eskimo*, 1961. New York: Fawcett. An explorer and adventurer discovers participant observation and becomes an amateur anthropologist.

Golde, Peggy, ed. *Women in the Field: Anthropological Experiences*, 2nd ed., 1986. Berkeley: University of California Press. Interesting reflections on the participant observation experience.

Hays, H.R. *From Ape to Angel: An Informal History of Social Anthropology*, 1958. New York: Capricorn Books. A lively and witty review of the lives and works of some key figures in the development of anthropology; includes a fine chapter on Schoolcraft.

Hoffman, Nicholas von and Sally W. Cassidy. "Interviewing Negro Pentecostals." *American Journal of Sociology*, 1956-57, 62:195-197. The account of two sociologists' adventures with participant observation; some excellent lessons for the field researcher working in our own society.

Jorgensen, Danny L. *Participant Observation: A Methodology for Human Studies*, 1989. Newbury Park, CA: Sage Publications. A succinct overview of the basic principles and strategies of participant observation; the author's intention is to provide an introduction to participant observation for those with no prior familiarity with the approach.

Lévi-Strauss, Claude. *Tristes Tropiques*, translated by John and Doreen Weightman, 1974. New York: Atheneum Publishers. One of the foremost contemporary anthropologists discusses, in a poetic and philosophical manner, what it means to do participant observation fieldwork.

Malinowski, Bronislaw. *Argonauts of the Western Pacific*, 1984 (original 1922). Prospect Heights, IL: Waveland Press. One of the classic ethnographies, by one of the giants of modern anthropology. In the first section in particular, Malinowski writes with lyric eloquence and perception about how it feels to do participant observation. This is one of the most influential statements about fieldwork in the history of anthropology.

Mead, Margaret. *Coming of Age in Samoa*, 1928. New York: William Morrow.

Mead, Margaret. *Growing Up in New Guinea*, 1930. New York: William Morrow.

Rabinow, Paul. *Reflections on Fieldwork in Morocco*, 1977. Berkeley: University of California Press. One of the most prominent exponents of "reflexive" anthropology (that which tries to understand the process of doing anthropology and the role of the individual anthropologist in the conduct of fieldwork) discusses his own participant observation experiences.

Spindler, George, ed. *Being an Anthropologist: Fieldwork in Eleven Cultures*, 1986 (original 1970). Prospect Heights, IL: Waveland Press. Reflections on how several anthropologists adapted to life in the field.

Spradley, James P. *Participant Observation*, 1980. New York: Holt, Rinehart and Winston. An interesting treatise on participant observation, written from the point of view of a specialist in ethnosemantic research (see Project 10).

Vidich, A. and J. Bensman. "The Validity of Field Work Data." *Human Organization*, 1954, 13(1): 20-27. The authors raise some sobering and thought-provoking questions as to possible sources of bias and misinformation that can arise out of the participant observation strategy.

Project Six

Collecting Life Histories

Every complete ethnography should give the reader an understanding of the life cycle of the people in question — what it is like to be born, to live each phase of life, and to die in that particular society. Obviously, much of the information that any anthropologist gathers in the field, because it is about a person or people, can be useful in illuminating portions of the life cycle. It may, of course, happen that during the anthropologist's year or so in a particular field situation no marriages, puberty ceremonies, or funerals take place. The information about such events must then be gathered by word of mouth only. Even if he or she is afforded an opportunity to observe such things, it will be important to elicit people's statements about the role of such events in their lives.

In a good summary article, David Mandelbaum (1973) speaks of anthropologists as having used two main approaches in their "observation of the development of a person." The first type, which he designates "life passage (or life cycle) studies," is seen as emphasizing the requirements of *society* and showing "how the group socialize and enculturate their young in order to make them into viable members of society." He points out that life-passage events have been studied in various cultures, and cross-cultural comparisons highlighting similarities and differences between societies in this regard have sometimes been very valuable. (As examples, he cites Arnold van Gennep's work on rites of passage [1909] and Margaret Mead's work on "coming of age" in Samoa [1928] and New Guinea [1930].) Such studies have, however, tended to emphasize a single stage of life, characteristically an early one.

The second type of approach Mandelbaum mentions is that of "life history studies," which emphasize the experience and requirements of the *individual*—how the individual copes with and develops within society (Mandelbaum 1973, p. 177). Such accounts, which follow an individual through the course of his or her career, are, of course, collected by people in many fields and familiar to us all as "biographies" and "autobiographies." In anthropological research, however, neither designation is really accurate, for the finished product is the result of collaboration between the subject and the anthropologist. Often the written document is set down by the anthropologist on the basis of verbal accounts by the subject. Often, too, the anthropologist must handle many problems of translation and interpretation when the subject speaks an exotic tongue or has little or no acquaintance with the written word, and he or she encounters problems of sequence of elicitation and presentation if the subject has no sense of chronology as we know it, and so on. For these reasons, the finished product, neither truly autobiographical nor biographical, is called a "life history" by anthropologists.

Most social scientists would strongly agree with Mandelbaum that, despite the fact that all anthropologists in the field gather a great deal of data that relate in one way or another to the "development of a person" in the society in question, there is little systematic collection and analysis of such data, and much too little attention is given to trying to combine life-passage data with life-history data from the same society in systematic and meaningful ways. Though life-passage studies have concentrated on children, life histories are almost exclusively of adults. Mandelbaum suggests that life-passage studies seldom effectively relate one stage of life to the next, personal experience to social institutions, or the exercise of personal choice to social change, although such matters are likely to be treated in a life history. With regard to life histories, he shows that, despite the urging of people in every branch of the social sciences, there have been all too few careful studies of lives as wholes, and that those that do exist lack commensurability, and often, adequate contextual treatment and careful analysis.

Pertti Pelto points out, in the spirit of Mandelbaum's suggestions, that life histories are sometimes collected by anthropologists specifically for the purpose of relating the details and abstractions of ethnographic description to the lives of individuals. He quotes Paul Radin, who stated that his aim in collecting his well-known biography of a Winnebago Indian was "not to obtain autobiographical details about some definite personage, but to have some representative middle-aged individual of moderate ability describe his life in relation to the social group in which he had grown up." Such detailed biographies of representative individuals can then be mined for the many kinds of information they provide, including descriptive material on the life cycle. A careful blending of the two types of materials enables the ethnographer to present an especially complete and well-rounded view of life in the society in question. We do not, of course, suggest that you create for this course the kind of extensive synthesis and analysis called for by Mandelbaum and others, but want to give you some understanding of the two types of studies, their interrelationships, and their importance. The remainder of this chapter is devoted solely to life-history studies.

In the few decades just before the first life histories were collected by anthropologists—and, in fact, before anthropologists were truly anthropologists—many events took place that played an important role in determining not only what early life histories would be like, but also what much of the nature and development of our discipline would be. Scientific knowledge of humans is, on the whole, amazingly recent, despite the fact that speculations about people, their origins, their differences in customs and ideas, seem to be as old as human thought. From the 1500s through the 1700s, the voyages of "discoverers" made the then-literate world increasingly aware of other peoples and their ways. So different did the "Indians" of the New World seem to the *conquistadores*, for example, that it became necessary for the Pope to issue a bull in the 1500s for the purpose of stating that Indians are human beings and are entitled to be treated as such. Even as late as the eighteenth century, Carolus Linnaeus, the great natural history systematizer, was led by the then-current beliefs to include in his classification of man not only *Homo sapiens* ("thinking man"), but also *Homo ferus* ("wild man"), and *Homo monstrosus* ("man monster"). Only very gradually did the strange creatures and mythical lands portrayed in tales and travelers' legends become discredited and relegated to limbo. Yet some mistaken notions lingered on, occasionally fostered by the managers of carnivals and sideshows who displayed a "wild man from Borneo" (who often bore little resemblance to anyone from that country).

By the early 1800s, however, the habit of precise observation was better established. Rumors and myths had been and were being checked up on. Large reservoirs of information about humans and their nature—physical and cultural—were being collected. Two important things came from this period: awareness of others who shared the fact of being human, and an awakening concern for those human creatures who were being exploited by their fellow humans. As people became increasingly aware of the predicament of the Tasmanians who were being shot down, of the treatment given black slaves in the Americas and elsewhere, and so on, they began to form humanitarian organizations to fight for their protection. It was in these same times and on the basis of these same concerns that the first anthropological and ethnological societies and journals came into being.

During this same period in the United States, where the great Indian wars were just ending and the frontiers were rapidly vanishing, there came to be great popular interest in Native Americans, especially in those chiefs or warriors who had achieved notice in some way. "This interest was, of course, of a romantic or sentimental kind and manifested itself mostly in written accounts of the 'noble savage,' the 'vanishing red man,' and similar tales" (Langness 1965, p. 5). In 1832 B.B. Thatcher published *Indian Biography: or, An Historical Account of Those Individuals Who Have Been Distinguished Among the North American Natives as Orators, Warriors, Statesmen and Other Remarkable Characters.* Artists and travellers began to supplement their Indian studies with brief biographies. In the later 1800s there appeared a series called *Famous American Indians*, and individual biographies of such famous Indians as Sitting Bull (1891), Black Hawk of the Sauk (1854), Pontiac of the Ottawa (1861), Brant of the Mohawk (1865), Chief Joseph of the Nez Perce (1881), Uncas of the Mohicans (1842), and Sequoya of the Cherokee (1885), to name a few (Langness, 1965, p. 5).

L. Langness, author of *The Life History in Anthropological Science* (1965), mentions biographies of Indians in the early 1900s which he groups with those mentioned above as "popular accounts." In summary he states, however, that "no real interest in biography as a specific tool for research had been shown by anthropologists" until the 1920s when Paul Radin published *Crashing Thunder*. In making this statement, he does not consider several brief biographical sketches by Grinnell, Kroeber, Wallis and others. Clyde Kluckhohn (1945) had previously called attention to the lack of anthropological use of the life history, and to the fact that any potential the early popular accounts possessed as sources of data had never been exploited by anthropologists.

Langness considers all of the other kinds of data with which anthropologists characteristically return from the field, and questions whether they alone can be an adequate substitute for an intensive life history. He concludes that while life histories were not considered truly mandatory in most anthropological studies seventy years ago, they had been becoming increasingly important ever since, especially in certain types of studies, such as those which emphasize personality and culture, the role of the individual in society, or developmental history. From the 1920s, then, there was some increase in attention being focused on the individual in society—not only in the United States but in Europe as well. In the United States, the focus in the first anthropological life histories, still called autobiographies by many of their collectors, continued to be on American Indians. In the 1930s Truman Michelson collected the "autobiographies" of three Indian women from different tribes—of special importance because they were early attempts to present the female side of what had remained a heavily male-oriented subject.

Looking back at the life histories that have been collected, Langness credits Edward Sapir and Paul Radin with having made the greatest and most enduring contributions to the field. He credits Sapir with having bridged the disciplines of psychology and psychiatry, as well as anthropology, greatly affecting the "school" of personality and culture, and influencing the work of Ruth Benedict, Ernest Beaglehole, and Walter Dyk (1967, p. 8). From Pelto's quotation given earlier, it can be seen that Radin's interest in life history materials was of a very different sort.

Although many scholars were engaged in work with American Indians between 1925 and 1945, most were oriented toward the idea that Indian cultures were fast disappearing and it was essential to salvage as many of them as possible. Life histories were not usually seen as a necessary part of the job, perhaps partly because they are more time-consuming than many other methods of data collection. The bulk of anthropological biography during the period was directed toward "clarifying or portraying the cultural dimension of human existence rather than the idiosyncratic or psychological dimension" (Langness 1965, p. 9). Among the most interesting and valuable studies of the period are Dyk's *Son of Old Man Hat* (1967) and Leo Simmons' *Sun Chief* (1942), as well as Radin's *Crashing Thunder*, mentioned earlier.

Langness summarizes the 1925-1945 period as showing an increasing interest in life histories and the methodology of life-history collection. He notes that since 1945 there has been a growing trend toward "less difficult methods of gathering data" (1965, p. 19). The life histories of the post-1945 period have, however, shown far greater diversity in the people chosen as subjects, as well as in the approaches utilized. The requests of many social scientists for greater numbers of carefully documented life histories still remain inadequately answered. The major inadequacies, aside from sheer numbers, include frequent lack of documentation to explain and give the setting for the study; very uneven representation of age and sex groups, with males over fifty as the vast majority of subjects; little contextual material and few life histories from the same group, hence little opportunity for comparison or judging how representative a particular life history is; and lack of analysis and interpretation.

Unlike the situation with so many other aspects of fieldwork, there simply was no good "how to" book about the collection of life histories. Now nearly fifty years old, the section by Kluckhohn in *The Use of Personal Documents in History, Anthropology, and Sociology* (1945), especially the section on "Field Techniques and Methods," was one of the first publications that gave some useful suggestions on the subject.

A primary suggestion of Kluckhohn's is that the collector of a life history should not depend solely upon reading about the community in question before starting interviews with a life-history informant. To select informants carefully and probably to establish sufficient rapport with them, the fieldworker should get a "feel" of the community from firsthand observation. The precise steps taken to do this will vary from place to place and with various situations. When one does not know a community well, it is also easy, as we mentioned earlier, to blunder into "touchy" topics or things that would be considered too personal and private. Often too, a bonus can come from looking at the whole community because the informant may then relax since he or she does not feel like the sole focus of attention. In your research for this project, it would be ideal if you were invited to visit in the informant's home. If such an invitation is not freely forthcoming on short acquaintance, perhaps you will be able to visit the informant at his or her work site, favorite sunny park bench, or another place where the informant will feel "at home," and you may be able to meet, or at least see, the informant's friends and acquaintances as he or she interacts with them. Wherever and whenever you visit your informant, always be sure that your presence is expected, not unwelcome, and not a hindrance to any other activity in which the informant is engaged.

The problem of motivating the informant can become a difficult one, as Kluckhohn reports from experience (p. 117), unless there is something about which the informant would like to let off steam, or something of which he or she is particularly proud. This is, of course, especially true if one wants to collect the whole of a lengthy and complicated tale and the informant is a busy person. Many people also consciously or unconsciously resent being "pumped dry." Kluckhohn (p. 115) hints it is a good idea to "prime the pump" by telling stories of one's own life, thus giving a feeling of sharing. In many situations, especially where the informant is an old acquaintance, it may be sufficient to ask something like "Won't you help me out with my work?" In other cases, the desire to help someone really know the truth about the community instead of "some of the lies about us in books" may be a strong motivating factor.

One thing that Kluckhohn emphasizes has particular relevance for the rather time-consuming business of gathering a life history. He points out that even if a particular person is a very desirable potential informant from the point of view of sampling, articulateness, and many other factors we have mentioned, he is usually "a bad risk if the inevitable pressures upon him to engage in other activities are strong and likely to be cumulative" (pp. 120-121). If such a person has agreed to be a life-history informant only to be helpful or friendly, but against his or her better judgment or that of influential family members, he or she may well have to cut short the interview, or may hurriedly telescope episodes so that they become lifeless and uninteresting. It is also important for the fieldworker to be sure he or she is seen as open and available. The authors have had the experience of having people literally knock on the door and volunteer to participate as subjects—very insightful ones—in a life-history project. Kluckhohn warns that the person who is "capricious or unstable or characterized by highly ephemeral enthusiasms" should be avoided unless he or she is especially needed as an informant (p. 121). The difficulties of detecting such qualities of temperament on short acquaintance are, of course, great, but the fieldworker should attempt to evaluate the nature and intensity of the motivation of subjects.

Kluckhohn suggests that certain aspects of the situation can be carefully structured by the investigator, with one eye on cultural conditions and the other on the informant's personality and motivations. Sometimes a third eye might be very useful! We mentioned earlier that if it is agreeable to the informant and in no way troublesome, it is good to conduct an interview in a place where the informant feels at home, and where one can see him or her in interaction with others. This is partly because it is very good to get an idea of the context of the informant's life and to add to one's knowledge, if possible, by speaking with others about things which concern the informant. There are, however, difficulties in controlling all of the factors involved. A friend of ours had established good rapport with a married couple over a considerable period. He asked the husband, who had always been a particularly willing, insightful, and articulate informant, to tell him his life story. When he arrived at the home at the appointed hour, he was greeted at the door by the wife, who kindly ushered him in. As they sat down to talk, however, she said, "I don't know what you want to interview him for. He's never done anything worth writing about. You should interview somebody who's had an interesting life!" This was undoubtedly meant as a show of modesty, but it effectively convinced the husband that he knew nothing worth saying. The interview was quickly completed; and the husband later reluctantly denied permission for it to be published in a group of life histories. Similar occurrences are frequent enough so that you should be on the lookout to prevent them. It might be necessary, for example, to conduct interviews in your own headquarters in the community if such a problem threatens.

Although some aspects of life-history interviewing are not clearly formulated and spelled out, there is one aspect about which everyone who has done extensive life-history interviewing is sure: the need to be at times a kind of "blank screen upon which the informant projects his life" (Kluckhohn, p. 122). The ethnographer should be as nondirective as possible, and, once the informant understands the task ahead, the ethnographer should say as little as possible. To interrupt may be to discourage, and the topic in question will probably never be returned to satisfactorily. One must be sensitive to the informant's reactions, but one should usually speak only to reassure or break a complete silence. It is, of course, exceedingly difficult to be both a blank screen and a friend, but this kind of approach may be necessary for the free flow of personal statement and the maintenance of essential support. More preliminary conversation and reassurance before the actual life history begins may, of course, be necessary if you do not know the informant well.

In life-history interviews the subject matter is somewhat personal, and the relationship between ethnographer and informant is never as cursory and simple as when some other information is gathered in the field. These are additional reasons why informants for life-history research should be chosen with special care. Kluckhohn speaks (p. 122) of the necessity for the anthropologist to build up a trust comparable to that enjoyed by a physician, lawyer, or priest, and to honor in every way the obligations involved. This is no small challenge, and must be taken seriously. The ethical responsibility for protecting the informant and his or her anonymity is of great importance, especially now that members of the community being studied are likely to read about themselves. It is important to try to get informants to agree to publication of their lives and to get others who will be affected also to agree to publication of what is being said about them. It is also true that publishers are reluctant to put out any life history for which permission has not been given by the informant—in writing, if possible.

Another important matter that Kluckhohn brings up is that of recording and keeping a verbatim record without stopping the informant—since rapport is almost always damaged unless the subject can select and maintain his or her own tempo (p. 127). Stenography or some forms of speedwriting are solutions he suggests, although today's mechanized anthropologist would also suggest a tape recorder. The length of an interview must be worked out carefully, since some informants tire quickly while others hate to break off.

When collecting life-history material, the ethnographer should always try to get as much information as possible from people other than the informant. In this way, one can pick up differences between the informant's conception of himself or herself and others' conceptions of the informant. It also serves as a check for information that the informant would be reluctant to give or has given incorrectly. It is also worthwhile, if possible, to obtain accounts by other eyewitnesses to events recounted in detail by the informant.

Although you will be asked to collect only one life history for this project and will, therefore, not be able to compare and contrast with other life histories from the same context, you might get some valuable insights by thinking about the product you collect from different points of view than those you originally planned. For example, is there use of ideas about the past, present and future? Are the people portrayed as important in the life of the same or different sexes, the same or different ages? Was the informant prodded to tell the story or eager to volunteer? Are there stylistic aspects of the story that stand out, such as narration techniques, humor, double entendre, irony, suspense or special beginnings and endings? Does the format of the story tend to resemble the format of some other stories with which the informant is familiar, such as those in religious services or meetings of Alcoholics Anonymous?

Recent writers tend to emphasize the idea that life histories can never tell of all the events in a person's life and are reflections of aspects of that person's "identity" that he or she chooses to present. We have been struck on some occasions with the clear and definite ideas some informants have about what constitutes their life stories even in places where the people have never before written a story or spoken into a tape recorder. Although the use of the tape recorder provides the illusion of first-person autobiography, the interaction of the interviewer and the informant is also of basic importance. "The interviewer and subject conspire to construct a version of the self—and the strategies they employ in that conspiracy will probably derive from the shared, unspoken regularities of interaction expectations in their culture" (Angrosino 1989, p. 104).

Over the past several years we have been making collections of life histories on several Dutch Caribbean islands. Our subjects on each island are proportionately representative of the ethnic groups found there, both sexes, and many occupational categories. They range in age from thirteen to the late eighties. Thus, we are attempting to make collections each of which is somewhat like the life history of an island. Though there are some similar themes running through the stories because the islands are all part of the same culture sphere, there are also many striking differences from island to island. The stories from Saba emphasize the proud heritage of the "Saba goats," inhabitants of a steep, isolated island, who managed to create a good life for themselves and to give rise to generations of seafaring men who are respected the world over for their skill. Stories from St. Eustatius often emphasize pride in being "sons and daughters of the soil" and in the African-American heritage. Stories from Aruba, an island whose population is made up of people from many nations, many of whom migrated there for the oil industry, often have as a main focus the rapid social change which has taken place in this cosmopolitan area. Thus, the life-history technique is a useful way to learn about many different kinds of societies — not just very traditional ones, or those whose culture is disappearing.

More important to mention here are some basic shifts in methodology which have been necessary along the way. The first project we conducted was on Saba, where one of us had previously lived and conducted research for some time. Therefore, it was possible to give the students who participated in that project some background before they arrived on the island and to "plug them in" with local people who became their first informants. As time went on, they found informants themselves among their new friends. On the other islands our ties were not as close or long-established as those on Saba, and we depended on friends in those islands to help us find and work with some of our informants. Although it helped that the friends who introduced us were highly respected locally, our relationships with the new acquaintances were of the kind that required much more initial friendly interaction and reassurance than was needed in the Saba project. In each case, the person was told that, contrary to their experience of our past research in the islands, we now intended to use real names, and their photos as well. In this way, of course, some "juicy tidbits" were lost; but everyone felt comfortable with the results.

One result of the life-history collections has been most important to us. We feel we have found at least a partial answer to a question our students sometimes ask: "But what do anthropologists do for the *people*?" We have found, as you may well find with the life histories you collect, that the subjects and their families often consider the stories family treasures. To our delight, when the central government gave each island an opportunity to choose which projects should be given grants from the cultural affairs funds, people on two of the islands, Saba and St. Eustatius, chose to nominate our life-history collections.

The Project

Collect the life history of an informant, bearing in mind the several suggestions from Kluckhohn. This is to be a nondirective interview, so that it is, as much as possible, the informant's own story in every way, emphasizing what he or she thinks is important to tell rather than what the questioner thinks is important to ask about. Thus, as soon as you are sure the informant understands what is wanted, you can begin with such nondirective questions as, "Please tell me about your life as a child," or "What was it like to grow up here in Blankville at the turn of the century?" (Despite their nondirective nature, such questions may well have been planned in advance.) This kind of interviewing may be useful for most of the collection of a life history with voluble and insightful informants. In most cases, however, other kinds of more directive, specific questions are necessary as well. We have found it especially rewarding to ask people who they consider to be the most important people, and what are the most important events in their lives. Please remember Kluckhohn's caution against interrupting your informant unless it is necessary to do so.

If the life history is collected in more than one session, it is a good idea to think out questions raised by the first session and to ask them of the informant in the next interview session, or in a brief visit for final questions. With informants who can manage to think through a chronology, it is wise to work out a year-by-year list of events as a check for the ordering of the items in the history.

We suggest, especially for those who have not worked with tape recorders, that this project might well be carried out on tape. This will provide experience not only in working with a "little black box" for interviewing but also in the time-consuming and demanding business of transcription. By this means, the student will also be better equipped to gauge the amount of material he or she will wish to record in fieldwork with future transcription time in mind. United States publications have recently suggested that one hour of tape translates into thirty typed pages. This may well be far more than you will have on an hourly basis from another society; but it is good to bear in mind that transcribing the words of people who speak languages or even dialects which are different from your native tongue may take far longer than working with texts in your own language. Accurate transcription is absolutely essential in life-history work, both because one must be faithful to the words and feelings of informants and because informants know when words are not *their* words and misquotes might well lead to refusal of permission to publish a life history.

When you write up and present your material, please remember all of the necessary ethical safeguards for your informant, including the possible necessity of giving the person a fictitious name, or otherwise hiding him or her, unless you have full permission to use the real name and all of the details in your story.

Selected Annotated Bibliography

Angrosino, Michael V. *Documents of Interaction: Biography, Autobiography and Life History in Social Science Perspective*, 1989. Gainesville: University Presses of Florida. Focuses on the critical nature of interaction between anthropologist and informant, writer and reader.

Bertaux, Daniel. *Biography and Society: The Life History Approach in the Social Sciences*, 1981. Newbury Park, CA: Sage Publications. Although the emphasis of this book is on applications in sociology, many useful ideas for all social sciences are included.

Casagrande, Joseph B., ed. *In the Company of Man: Twenty Portraits of Anthropological Informants*, 1960. New York: Harper. The twenty life histories recorded by well-known anthropologists are fascinating reading in themselves, and also give insights into the ethnographer-informant relationship in producing a life history.

Crane, Julia G., ed. *Saba Silhouettes*, 1987. New York: Vantage. A collection of life histories from a single island.

Dyk, Walter. *Son of Old Man Hat: A Navaho Autobiography*, 1967. Lincoln: University of Nebraska Press. Lively, fascinating reading. Thoroughly recommended.

Kluckhohn, Clyde. "The Personal Document in Anthropological Science." In L. Gottschalk, C. Kluckhohn and R. Angell, eds., *The Use of Personal Documents in History, Anthropology, and Sociology*, 1945. Social Science Research Council, Bulletin 53, pp. 78-173. Although more than forty years old, this is still a valuable and helpful collection of ideas and suggestions.

Langness, L.L. *The Life History in Anthropological Science*, 1965. New York: Holt, Rinehart and Winston. A good little manual on the uses of life-history material. Ample bibliographic treatment.

Mandelbaum, David G. "The Study of Life History: Gandhi." *Current Anthropology*, 1973, 14(3):177-196. A review of life-history research, with additional suggestions on creating life histories based upon literature rather than interviews.

Mead, Margaret. *Coming of Age in Samoa*, 1928. New York: William Morrow.

Mead, Margaret. *Growing Up in New Guinea*, 1930. New York: William Morrow. Two of Mead's pioneering works, both emphasizing children and adolescents. Many new editions are available.

Pelto, Pertti J. and Gretel H. Pelto. *Anthropological Research: The Structure of Inquiry*, 2nd ed., 1978. Cambridge, England: Cambridge University Press. A carefully prepared treatment on a great many types of anthropological research—little treatment is actually given to life histories.

Radin, Paul. *The Autobiography of a Winnebago Indian*. University of California Publications in American Archaeology and Ethnology, 1920, 16:381-473. Subsequently published as *Crashing Thunder*, 1963. Mineola, NY: Dover Publications. Still good reading.

Simmons, Leo W. *Sun Chief, The Autobiography of a Hopi Indian*, 1942. New Haven, CT: Yale University Press. Probably ranks with *Son of Old Man Hat* as one of the most fascinating to read.

Van Gennep, Arnold. *Les Rites de Passage*, 1900. Paris: Libraire Cortique, Emile Nouray. Translated, 1960. Chicago: University of Chicago Press. The classic work on puberty ceremonies.

Project Seven

Using Personal Documentation

An anthropologist in the field ordinarily gathers information through observation and by some form of direct interviewing. Any time an informant tells anything to the anthropologist, the latter is collecting "personal documentation," but for the purposes of this chapter, we can restrict that term and apply it mainly to extended narrative accounts of the informant's life, experiences, or opinions.

By far the most commonly used form of personal documentation is the life history, described in Project 6. The life history is most frequently collected by the interviewer in person, but if one is working in a literate society it is also possible to collect diaries or autobiographical essays that serve the same purpose. Such a method has the advantage of providing information from a wider circle of people than those who could be interviewed in person.

Most of the anthropologists who have made use of this technique have tended to rely on some existing group, such as secondary-school students, for whom the writing of an essay might be considered part of the normal course of events. In many communities, adults are not accustomed to writing more than an occasional letter, and might feel threatened by the request to write something fairly elaborate. A possible means of overcoming such reluctance might be to ask the adults to keep running diaries of brief jottings, rather than to write full-blown prose narratives. Such diaries have been used extensively by psychologists dealing with individual case histories, but they can also be employed profitably by anthropologists studying group activity. Essays and diaries can be used to elicit information on a wide variety of subjects. Information on any topic that could be the subject of a personal interview could also be written down by a literate informant.

There are two main categories of information for which such a technique seems particularly appropriate. When one is interested in outlining the daily round of activities, the diaries of informants (whether they are in constant contact with the fieldworker or are somewhat peripheral to the circle of key informants) can provide a picture of the mundane events that fill the days of people in the community. Becase people will fill diaries with what they consider important, a study of informants' diaries can give a very good indication of what those in a particular culture feel to be significant in the world around them, as opposed to what the researcher perceives to be important based on an outsider's perspective. By comparing several of these accounts, the anthropologist can come to some conclusions about the "typical" course of life. To do so is not merely to catalog mundane events, but also to come to an understanding of how the people themselves feel about the events of their lives.

On the other hand, the fieldworker is often especially interested in eliciting statements on values and attitudes. In the American school of cultural anthropology, the study of shared values receives important emphasis; indeed most commonly held definitions of culture include some indication of the value system of the people, in addition to the things that they make, do, or create. Individuals, to be sure, will value different things, and hold different opinions on a variety of issues, but there are certain attitudes that will be fairly common to the members of a given society. These are the attitudes that help to hold that society together, because they represent areas in which a diversity of individual interests can come together in agreement.

In anthropological literature, one finds a bewildering array of terms — "sentiments," "values," "patterns," "themes," "premises," and so on — that refer to constellations of shared ideas and attitudes. We need not become involved in definitional problems here, because, for the purposes of this project, all these related concepts can be spoken of in Ralph Linton's terms as "anything which has meaning for two or more of a society's component members" (Linton 1936, p. 422).

A society stays together only as long as its members are in some sort of general agreement as to what they are doing and what they are striving toward.

> A stable social structure prevails only so long as the majority
> of individuals in the society find enough satisfaction both in the
> goals socially approved and in the institutionalized means of
> attainment to compensate them for the constraints which
> ordered social life inevitably imposes upon uninhibited response
> to impulse. In any way of life there is much that to an outside
> observer appears haphazard, disorderly, more or less chaotic.
> But unless most participants feel that the ends and means of
> their culture make sense, disorientation and amorality become
> rampant (Kluckhohn & Leighton 1974, pp. 295-296).

One way an anthropologist can better understand the areas of
agreement that hold any particular society together is to see how
often statements of such values turn up in the discourse of the
people, and then to see in what contexts they turn up. However, since
people do not always verbalize the values by which they guide their
lives, it is often charged that anthropologists are too vague when
they try to report such matters. Getting informants to verbalize their
own attitudes, then, is one of the reasons for the use of personal
documentation.

An example of the use of personal documentation concerns the
island of Saba, a tiny island in the northern part of the Lesser
Antilles (the long arc of small islands in the Caribbean), which is
politically affiliated with the Netherlands. Saba is essentially a single
steep volcanic peak. Until recent years there was no way for ships
to land there because of the pounding surf and the lack of protected
harbors. Even air service was impossible until the 1960s because
of the lack of level landing space. As a result, Saba people
characteristically emigrated if they chose to pursue the economic
and social benefits offered by the world outside. "The young people
of Saba believe it is good to emigrate," an ethnographer may say.
But how do we know? Obviously, a survey questionnaire would take
us only so far. For example, an ethnographer asked young people
in Saba the question: "Would you like to live the main part of your
life in Saba or some other country?" The former statement could
then be revised to say, "All but one of the forty-five respondents over
twelve years of age said that they would prefer to spend the main
parts of their lives in some other place" (Crane 1971, p. 197). But
even so, we would know very little about *why* young people plan
to leave or what this orientation to emigration means to the society.

A collection of short autobiographies written by schoolchildren
gives a clearer picture of how deeply the idea of emigration is rooted
in the culture. Moreover, by examining the context in which
emigration is mentioned in the autobiographies, we can learn more
about why people plan for and expect it. Because the statements

are in their own words, we can get some of the tone of feeling surrounding emigration as well. Four young people wrote as follows:

> I'd like to go America to school because I have family there. Because when you become a woman there isn't any work here for anybody to do. So if you want to earn money the best thing is to go away and earn a living or if you're still young to go to school until you're old enough. Because your father and mother do not live forever. And they will not be here to support you.

> I would not like to stay on Saba. Because there is no future for boys and girls. I want to go to Aruba. Where I can finish school. On Saba you can't go nowhere. Sometimes swimming on a Sunday, or to the movies. But I seldom go.

> I don't want to remain always on Saba. I want to go to Aruba or Curacao. I don't want to stay here because all you can do is to work in the ground or keep cattle.

> I do not want to remain always in Saba. Well you see Saba is small and doesn [sic] have nothing to interest you and after you have been in a place so long you don't find it so interrested [sic]. Well I can't say where I want to go, because there are so many places I want to go but when you are poor you can't do any better. So that is all (Cranc 1971, pp. 198-199).

It is an anthropological truism that behaviors that appear similar occur in many parts of the world, but the connotations and implications of those behaviors may vary widely. For example, a study was undertaken in five communities in the southwestern United States: Zuñi and Navajo Indians, Spanish-Americans, Texas homesteaders, and Mormons (Kluckhohn and Strodtbeck 1961). All five communities were within several miles of one another and had to cope with the same ecological problems. Yet because of the distinct value systems from which the groups operated, each community came up with different "answers" to the same sorts of problems. Farming, for example, meant a link to the past and to the ancestors as far as the Zuñi were concerned. For the Texas homesteaders it meant a stake in the future and a break with the Dust Bowl hardships of the past. Thus, the same activity had two separate meanings, depending on the cultural context in which it occurred. Personal documentation analysis can sort out the contextual meaning of such behaviors and establish the cultural dimensions of a particular value or attitude. Moreover, the anthropologist can compare what people say they think and do, or plan to do, with their actual behavior. Doing so may help gain some insight into the differences between ideal culture and real culture.

The source of the anthropologist's assertion that "the young people of Saba believe it is good to emigrate" is ordinarily knowledge of the community derived from participant observation. We assume that numerous people who have reputations for honesty and reliability have said so repeatedly to the fieldworker. However, if it is possible to have those same sentiments written down by the informants themselves, that statement can be more readily quantified. In addition, the exact words of informants can be used for illustrative purposes, a very important consideration when preparing a full ethnographic report from field research.

Personal documentation is not the only source of such information. Some fieldworkers have had success in providing informants with cameras and asking them to take pictures of "good things" or "important people." Such a method, however, is not always practical in terms of budgetary considerations. Other anthropologists prefer to cross-check value statements by the use of standardized projective tests like the Rorschach and Thematic Apperception Test; but as these instruments require a great deal of specialized study to administer and interpret, fieldworkers should not rely on them.

The British anthropologist John Beattie feels that obtaining ". . . written statements either dictated by the informant to the anthropologist or his assistant and written down by him verbatim, or written down directly by the informant himself, is a vitally important part of modern fieldwork" (Beattie 1965, p. 30). Indeed, his ethnography of the Bunyoro Kingdom in East Africa is studded with such personal accounts, giving it a very intimate flavor. One of Beattie's innovations was to organize two essay competitions, to which both schoolchildren and other literate members of the community were invited. The Nyoro people, he found, had a flair for describing their culture — particularly its more esoteric aspects, such as sorcery and spirit mediumship — in prose form, although they ordinarily do not write such things down. As a result, he learned a great deal about Bunyoro that he might never have uncovered through verbal interviews alone.

Beattie sent a circular letter to the various locations where the people were living, explaining that he had come to their country to learn the "rules and customs of Bunyoro-Kitara both of long ago and those of today" (Beattie 1965, p. 31). He invited all interested people to write what they knew about certain topics. Cash prizes were offered for the best essays as an added incentive.

In general, Beattie called for topics he knew to be important in the culture, but about which he lacked information. He also called for a "residual" category, to allow people to write on other topics they felt to be important and that he might not have thought of himself. In the second competition, begun toward the end of his field study, he asked more focused questions and called for essays on topics for which he required certain specific data (Beattie 1965, pp. 30-37).

Vera Rubin and Marisa Zavalloni (1969) set out to study the attitudes of children in a Third World country. Everyone talks about the impact of modernization in the Third World, and most people agree that it is the educated youth of those areas who feel that impact most directly. The Rubin-Zavalloni study, set on the island of Trinidad in the West Indies, concentrated primarily on survey questionnaires to sort out aspects of the modernization experience as they affected the young people. But one of the survey instruments allowed the youngsters to write short essays in lieu of checking off responses. The young people were asked to write about their plans, expectations, and hopes beginning at the time of the study and going up to the year 2000. The students were told that if they did not wish to write their own "future autobiographies" they could write one for an imaginary subject of their own age and position (p. 210). One brief example:

> My family has a little plot of sugar cane which does not yield as before because the strength of the land is failing and the scientific methods which they have is too expensive, because he has a very little holding. I can then try to help my village as a whole, for it is a little one, but it has much potential and future. I can try and see that any factories or plants be opened up in my little village where the younger men would be able to get good jobs, and the little village could be made a very good one for any one to live in. If I become an influential man I can try to have any colleges or institutes not far from my area, so that it would be cheaper for the poor village peasants to get in their children without much trouble and expense (p. 165).

The frequency with which similar themes of economic development as the key to all kinds of happiness recur (including the benefits of education and political "influence") seems to indicate that the children see the growing disparity between the new, modernized elite (who are involved in the incipient industries of the island) and the old rural peasantry as the most troublesome aspect of culture change. This statement, general though it is, is certainly far stronger than the simple assertion that "children in the Third World are troubled by modernization and feel alienated from their traditional cultures."

On Trinidad's sister island, Tobago, a young Englishman named Chris Searle learned an important anthropological lesson by using something of the same tactic. He was faced with the contradictions of a situation in which he, a white man, was teaching black children about "their" heritage—actually the heritage of the colonial authorities—and he was concerned lest he impose too much of his own experience on them, and thereby fail to encourage them to realize what was unique in their own social and cultural heritage. He therefore began to collect samples of written work from his students, since in writing the children seemed to be less shy about revealing themselves than they were in conversation. Searle then analyzed these stories and poems in order to find out what the dominant themes were in these children's lives in order to understand their own particular "world view" better.

For one small example, Searle tackled the theme of the "island." In the minds of Europeans and North Americans, "the island" has traditionally symbolized escape, romance, glamour, adventure. But the black children, whose ancestors had been brought to the "island paradise" in chains, see it as an increasingly inconsequential dot on the map of the great, white world beyond. Tobago often connotes a place of isolation and imprisonment. The children feel that they are all "forsaken," and must accept the "guilt" for the "aloneness and forsakenness of the black children in the white world."

> Advantages of living on an island are, in an island their [sic] will not be much violence, discrimination as in the countries. In an island the people there will have to work hard at their jobs whether it is working in a garden or in a store.

> Most of the people there will be hard working people and when they work for a few cents, all will spend to feed and clothe a family. Rich people will not mistreat their servants. If someone is working for some one they will be treated kindly.

> In an island there will be peace and hardly any noise. The most noise you may here [sic] is from the animals playing in bushes. There will not be many kidnapping many road deaths and sad scenes.

> Children who live on an island will be healthy, cheerful children, they will be contented and grow up obedient and hard working in both work and schooling.

> On some island there will be lovely beaches with palm trees and coconut trees. Most of the trees and shrubs will be there and an artist could make a good scenery there. Tourism will go on on an island because there will be quietness, and peace and thats what tourist likes. They also come to see the beautiful flowers in bloom.

People will be welcome with hospitality on an island more than in a city. There will be pleasant smiles and friendly and cheerful greetings as they pass you. They [sic] won't be much haughtiness and quarrels about who has more money . . . (Searle 1972, pp. 16-17).

Despite the chins-up attitude of the thirteen-year-old authoress, she already knows that the quietness and flowers are for the tourists, and the hard work is for the natives: the best the latter can hope for is to be "treated kindly" as servants. Tobago is billed as "Robinson Crusoe's isle," and is a popular tourist destination, an economic boom that makes peace and quiet even harder to find, and that therefore alienates the island's inhabitants even more from their homeland.

The Project

Your project is to analyze a body of personal documents for clues to the sociocultural setting of which they are a part. For convenience, you should select a relatively small group of no more than ten individuals as your sample population. This size will, of course, restrict the number of generalizations you can legitimately make from the data, but it should be sufficient to enable you to see what sorts of inferences can be made.

If you have access to a school class (primary or secondary), it might be a logical place to start. You can, however, select the ten individuals at random, as long as they are linked in some way that might lead you to believe they would be able to express ideas about a common topic. Ten people who happen to get on a bus at the same time would not be a suitable group. Members of a college class, a political or social club, a religious congregation, or an ethnic or racial group might all be possible subjects. If your instructor agrees, you can combine this project with one or more of the others; for example, you can use the same congregation members who are your subjects in the Participant Observation project.

Your directions to these individuals should be rather general. The technique of asking them to write their autobiographies projected forward for twenty-five years is effective if you are dealing with adolescents, but it could be depressing or offensive to older people. A neutral topic, then, might be suggested, such as "Life in Our Town," "Trends in Campus Life," or "What Our Church Is Like."

The topic should be something that the informants are reasonably interested in and about which they have something to say, and it should be open enough to allow them to speak freely about what is really on their minds. Be sure that you explain to the informants that their names will not be used in anything you write about your study, and that you are not concerned about such things as grammar and spelling. Encourage them to be frank.

You may, if you have extra time, ask for a second series of essays, on more specific topics that have been suggested by the responses to the first collection. In any case, once you have your essays, you can analyze them much as you would any other textual material, such as folklore (see Project Nine). You should be primarily concerned with the recurring themes of these essays, since such themes are likely to define the areas of "common interest" that express the values of the culture that the informants share. Your information will probably fall into two broad categories:

• specific information (data on the culture)

• statements of ideas and attitudes, reflecting the way people respond to those "facts of life"

What are the points of agreement between the two in the individual essays? What are the themes that run through most or all of the essays? Most important, what is the "cultural meaning" behind the various facts of the culture—how, for example, do the informants feel about doing a certain thing?

Selected Annotated Bibliography

Angrosino, Michael V. "The Psychomedical Case Study of an East Indian Trinidad Alcoholic." *Ethos*, 1989, 17:202-225. Although it deals with only a single informant, this article demonstrates the way in which personal documents can be used to illustrate the relationship between people and their culture.

Beattie, John. *Bunyoro: An African Kingdom*, 1960. New York: Holt, Rinehart and Winston. This is an ethnography that depends in part on personal documentation.

Beattie, John. *Understanding an African Kingdom: Bunyoro*, 1965. New York: Holt, Rinehart and Winston. An interesting account of how one anthropologist went about his fieldwork; includes some valuable information on the use of documentation.

Crane, Julia G. *Educated to Emigrate: The Social Organization of Saba*, 1971. Assen, Netherlands: Royal van Gorcum. The ethnography of a Caribbean island; information was gathered in part through children's essays.

Kluckhohn, Clyde. "The Personal Document in Anthropological Science." In L. Gottschalk, C. Kluckhohn and R. Angell, eds., *The Use of Personal Documents in History, Anthropology, and Sociology,* 1945. Social Science Research Council, Bulletin 53, pp. 78-173. A standard survey of the field.

Kluckhohn, Clyde and Dorothea Leighton. *The Navaho,* 1974. Cambridge, MA: Harvard University Press.

Kluckhohn, Clyde, et al. "Values and Value Orientations in the Theory of Action: An Exploration in Definition and Classification." In T. Parsons and E. Shils, eds., *Toward a General Theory of Action,* 1967. Cambridge, MA: Harvard University Press. This is an often-cited example of the anthropological usage of the concepts dealt with in this project.

Kluckhohn, Florence, Fred L. Strodtbeck. *Variation in Value Orientations,* 1961. Evanston, IL: Row, Peterson. A comparative study of values in five Southwestern communities.

Leighton, Alexander H. *My Name is Legion,* 1959. New York: Basic Books. Appendix A (pp. 395-420) is a comprehensive review of the concepts of sentiment, value, etc., as used in the various social sciences. The accompanying bibliography is valuable for locating some of the older, less commonly used sources.

Linton, Ralph. *The Study of Man,* 1936. Norwalk, CT: Appleton-Century-Crofts. A classic introduction to anthropology; many of Linton's definitions — as of "value" and "interest" in this project — have become standard among American anthropologists.

Rubin, Vera and Marisa Zavalloni. *We Wish to Be Looked Upon: A Study of the Aspirations of Youth in a Developing Society,* 1969. New York: Teachers College Press. An exhaustive study of the attitudes of school children on the island of Trinidad. The appendices contain the survey questionnaires and essay instructions used to glean these data on values and attitudes.

Searle, Chris. *The Forsaken Lover: White Words and Black People,* 1972. London: Routledge and Kegan Paul. A young Englishman, a teacher in a school on the West Indian island of Tobago, learned about the "values and attitudes" of his students through their essays and poems, which he collected and interpreted in this volume.

Project Eight

Digging Into Cultural History

Anthropology includes within its scope an emphasis upon the history of human development. Clearly, historical research can provide important insights for understanding culture. A culture is to a great extent conditioned by what it has been, and it is not possible to understand fully what is occurring in the present, or why it is occurring, without reference to the past. In fact, the British anthropologist R. R. Marrett once declared that "anthropology is history or it is nothing."

The fact that we now have a much fuller picture of the past is in large measure a result of anthropological research. Anthropologists do differ, however, in the degree to which they value the historical perspective. Some social anthropologists, for example, concentrate almost entirely on comparing cultures existing at the same time. Nevertheless, contributions to understanding the past come from all four major subdivisions of the discipline. The ethnographer, the kind of anthropologist on whose work we are concentrating most in this volume, characteristically gives time depth and a broader perspective to research by interviewing people of all ages about their lives, by gathering these people's recollections of the lives of their ancestors, by studying any documents that may be available locally or in centralized archives, and so on.

Archaeologists are, of course, especially committed to the discovery of the past. The word archaeology comes from the Greek and means, literally, "the study of old things." It involves the recovery, study, and reconstruction of the past of humankind — processes that must be carried out both scientifically and

98

imaginatively. Anthropological archaeologists have characteristically interested themselves in digging up and interpreting the material remains of culture from the vast periods of the past for which there is no written history. Recently, however, many of them, particularly in the United States, have worked on historic sites as well as those representing prehistoric periods.

It is often possible to gain experience in archaeology by taking part in an authentic excavation (a "dig") or by working in the laboratory with artifacts found in the field. Skill in archaeological fieldwork comes mostly from doing it, not from reading about it. A very important caution to insert here is that if you are aware of a place where, for example, arrowheads or pieces of Indian pottery are being found, it should be reported to your state archaeologist. To dig a site is to destroy it, so the only people who should ever conduct a dig are those well trained in archaeological techniques. Only trained archaeologists can create, as they dig, all of the meticulous records that preserve knowledge of how the earth and the materials it contained were arranged in relationship to one another. When treasure-hunters find something that interests them and take it from the earth, they are ignoring its context. All of the earth and objects around artifacts, and the way those artifacts are associated with one another, could provide the clues an archaeologist needs to determine their dates and functions in the former society.

A great deal of effort has gone into developing systematic techniques for preserving more and more material remains from sites, and for recording more exactly the positions of objects and features found in a dig. Obviously, fishhooks, seed baskets, and arrowheads can reveal something about how a people made their living. But one or two of each can tell little of a culture. It is only when the archaeologist knows, for example, that there were once many fishhooks and few arrowheads in use by the people of an area, and that later there were many arrowheads and few fishhooks, that he or she can say hunting was becoming comparatively more important in the local economy and fishing less so. It is the context that provides the information archaeologists must have to reconstruct a culture. Their later conclusions about an ancient culture depend upon performing careful and scientific excavations. They may be aided in analysis by scientists in other fields, such as botanists and zoologists, whose specialized knowledge of plants, pollen, horns, shells, bone, and so forth can be essential in rounding out the total picture.

Some older texts speak of archaeologists as the "glamour boys of anthropology." (Today they would say "glamour persons.") To the extent that this is true, it is partly because the people being studied are forever beyond our reach, so that the archaeologist must bring considerable knowledge and skill to the work—as well as a less glamourous trait, self-discipline. Like detectives, archaeologists want to learn about people and their behavior; yet the only clues to the people studied may well exist solely in hidden objects and the marks in the soil that they are able to discover and analyze. Unfortunately, the passage of time and the ravaging effects of changing climate constantly destroy remains. The substances most resistant to decay are stone, metal, and pottery. Organic substances like shell, bone, antler, and wood are much more susceptible to decay. The poorest environment for preservation of organic material is the hot, moist jungle, where archaeologists sometimes find that all traces of organic material have disappeared within only five years. Whatever the conditions of preservation, archaeologists must work with what they can find. This is often a tantalizingly small portion of the original material remains (Gorenstein 1965, pp. 20-23).

While the archaeologist is interested in any valid evidence about the past of humankind, most of the evidence, as we have suggested, is to be found beneath the earth's surface. *Stratigraphy*, the observation of the earth's layers, or strata, is an important foundation for the study of the past. The use of stratigraphy in archaeology developed out of the pioneering work of geologists during the late eighteenth and early nineteenth centuries. (It is believed that Thomas Jefferson was the first person in the New World to conduct a dig that utilized these ideas.) One well-known British archaeologist has stated that the basis of scientific excavation is the carefully observed and accurately recorded stratigraphic profile.

Stratigraphy is based upon the simple principle that the upper layers of anything will have been placed there more recently than the lower layers. If, for example, you were to walk into a room and find that the baby of the family had piled blocks one on top of the other, you would know that the upper blocks were placed on the pile after the lower blocks. Unless you had been watching the baby, however, you have no way of knowing how much later the upper blocks were added. This is an example of relative dating, because we know only that the placement of some blocks was relatively later in time than the placement of others. In archaeology, unless the area has been very much disturbed, the digger can assume that, as he or she works down, each successively lower layer with the materials it contains will be older than the layers above. (See Figure 8-1.)

Although stratigraphic observation is only one of the principles that guide the archaeologist's trowel, we have chosen to mention it because of its basic importance in revealing sequences of prehistoric cultural changes. Under ideal conditions, sequences of evidence for cultural change may be found in clearly distinguishable layers at a stratified site. There are, however, many cases where conditions are far from ideal and no layering can be detected. In other cases, the materials we want to arrange in time sequence may not be found buried in the earth at all.

To ascertain cultural changes where stratigraphic evidence is unclear or lacking, archaeologists use *seriation*. Seriation is based on the idea that cultures change over time. By arranging something such as pottery or tomb types in sequences on the basis of degree of similarity, the archaeologist can arrive at a time sequence. The method was developed in 1902 by an Egyptologist who wanted to arrange a number of early tombs in time sequence. He worked out the sequence by studying the groups of pots placed with the skeletons. One particularly helpful clue was the nature of jar handles, which changed from useful extensions of the jars to more decorative handles, and later into mere painted lines.

As in jar handles, fashions come and go, which is obvious when we think of clothing styles, men's haircuts, high tailfins on auto-mobiles, or crazes like hula hoops. Successions of technological advances in the historical periods of Western society have also followed one another in rather rapid succession, especially when seen in terms of the whole sweep of human development.

Figure 8-2 illustrates the changes in devices for artificial lighting that took place in Pennsylvania between 1850 and 1950. It is a clear example of an application of the seriation method. The succession of types seems obvious to us because we are somewhat aware of the history of such things. But an archaeologist working with pottery types may, at first, not know what the sequence of the types was like. Working out a sequence of types is only one step in seriation. The next step is to work out the frequency of each type of object at each site where it was found. As one type grows in popularity and forms a large proportion of the material culture, others decrease in frequency. When archaeologists have worked out the pattern of increase and decrease of each type, they have the relative chronological position of each of the sites from which the sample came. To use the lighting fixture example, for which we know the chronology, if a site in the Upper Ohio Valley yielded 80 percent incandescent electric lamps, 10 percent gas lamps, and 5 percent kerosene lamps, it would suggest that the site was more recent than one that yielded a sample of 20 percent incandescent electric lamps, 65 percent gas lamps, and 10 percent kerosene lamps.

For archaeologists working with pottery types, the seriation method means arranging and rearranging the data on the various

Figure 8–1

South Profile

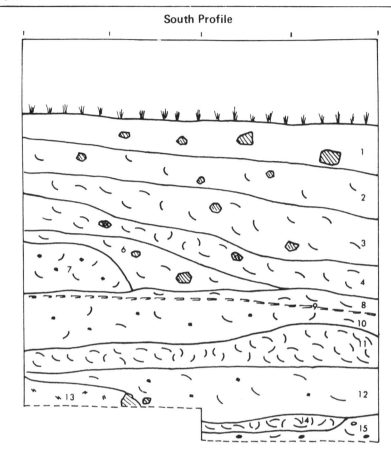

1. Topsoil, plow zone

2. Transitional zone

3. Grey-brown loam/ash
   powder

4. Light brown
   compacted loam

5. Loose brown loam

6. Grey-brown
   compacted loam

7. Dark brown-black lens

8. Brown-black layer

SECTION DRAWINGS   SITE 1A, PIT 2

Source: From Donald L. Brockington, "Archaeological Investigations at Miahuatlan, Oaxaca," 1973, by permission of *Vanderbilt University Publications in Anthropology*. Drawn by Maria Jorrin.

Chart illustrating stratigraphic profiles of an archaeological site.

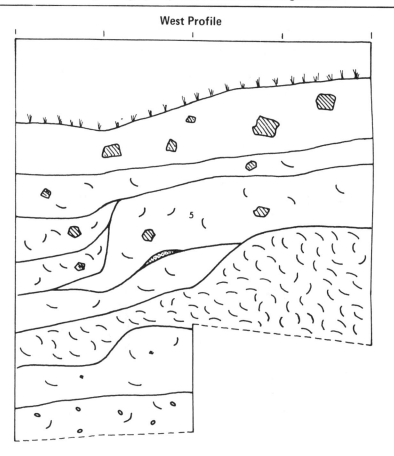

West Profile

9. Broken stucco floor

10. Light brown sandy loam

11. Light brown sandy loam with sherd concentration

12. Grey loam/ash with sherd concentration

13. Dark brown clay

14. Grey loam/ash powdered with sherd concentration

15. Compact sterile clay with limestone inclusions

Figure 8–2

Chart illustrating the seriation method

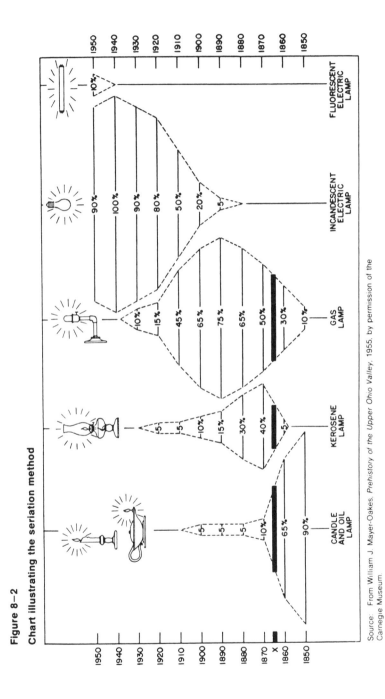

Source: From William J. Mayer-Oakes, *Prehistory of the Upper Ohio Valley,* 1955, by permission of the Carnegie Museum.

samples. The position of each sample on their chart represents its position in a time scale, so the archaeologists gradually develop the relative chronology of all of the sites in question (Gorenstein 1965, pp. 113-114).

Even if you cannot join a dig or work with a collection of material from one, you can use published evidence to carry on research into culture history. Kroeber and Richardson (1940), for example, once carefully analyzed style variations in European women's clothing for a three-hundred year period. They found that styles seem to be influenced by factors about which people are not even aware and that style changes occur in cycles, despite the efforts of designers and manufacturers. Not only did dress dimensions in general fluctuate in an orderly fashion, but each of the specific measures, such as waist height or fullness of skirt, had its own periodicity. As each dimension became more and more unlike the most characteristic form of that dimension, the probability that it would reverse directions increased. In times of peace and prosperity, dresses featured fitted bodices, full skirts, and natural waistlines. In times of war or economic depression, women wore extreme styles, with very high or very low waistlines, and skirts that were either short or narrow or both. Changes of style often took place during periods of stress. Kroeber concluded that, "since the periods of dress-pattern instability were also periods of marked sociopolitical instability and churning, there is presumably a connection" (1948, p. 334).

In "What Goes Up, May Stay Up," Marvin Harris (1973) reexamined the study by Kroeber and Richardson and updated it. He believes that the basic patterns they ascertained had begun to break up in 1913. As for dress length, Kroeber and his co-author had stated, "the upper limit of possibility and probably our less definable limits of decency" had been reached at the knee. Harris concludes, "They were right in one sense: By surging over the knee the basic pattern had oscillated itself right out of existence" (p. 24). He agrees with *Vogue*'s statement that "we are past being hung up on hemlines," and predicts that Western women "will never again tolerate a fashion that requires them to wear ankle-to-floor length skirts except as entirely optional alternatives to pants or short skirts. The demise of the floor-length skirt is the Occidental equivalent of the end of foot binding in China. . . ." (p. 24).

Other imaginative studies in culture history of which you may be aware include tracing the styles and inscriptions of gravestones and recent looks at the evolution of messages on bumper stickers.

The Project

1. Using several Sears, Roebuck catalogs, trace the history of two different classes of items from different major categories, such as men's boots, lighting fixtures, children's toys, women's bathing suits, or communications equipment. If you do not have access to old or reprinted Sears, Roebuck catalogs (which should be available at most libraries), you might consider working with a sample of issues of some long-established magazine such as *Good Housekeeping*, using either articles or advertisements or both. Analyze the changes that have taken place in the various members of your two classes of artifacts over time. Include in your analysis such things as when new traits appear and when traits disappear.

2. Archaeologists should not attempt to make sweeping generalizations on the basis of tracing changes in only a few classes of artifacts. They do, however, as we suggested, depend a great deal on the information provided by context in making interpretations. Using the same catalog or magazine issues you used for the first portion of the project, suggest some of the ways they provide contextual information about changes in the culture that might aid your interpretation of the changes in the classes of artifacts you examined. For example, does your "contextual material" provide clues about technological changes, periods of economic boom or recession, periods of war or peace, changes in orientation to rural or urban life, changes in the nature and use of leisure time, or changes in the nature of social relations? Note that one of the things upon which you might focus for suggestions is the people pictured, including the size of family groups implied, and so on.

Selected Annotated Bibliography

Clark, J. G. D. *Archaeology and Society: Reconstructing the Prehistoric Past*, rev. ed., 1970. New York: Barnes and Noble. First published, 1939, London: Methuen & Co. A well-done study, reprinted several times, concentrates on the Old World.

Daniel, Glyn. *The Origins and Growth of Archaeology*, 1967. Harmondsworth, Middlesex, England: Penguin Books. Just what it claims to be, including many short sketches on archaeologists and their major accomplishments. The emphasis is on European scholars.

Deetz, James. *Invitation to Archaeology*. 1967. Garden City, NY: American Museum Science Books, The Natural History Press. One of many good, basic treatments. Unlike those listed above, this book includes considerable New World material. Inexpensive and convenient, a true "pocket book."

Fagan, Brian M. *In the Beginning: Introduction to Archaeology*, 7th ed., 1991. New York: HarperCollins. One of the many introductory treatments, it provides liberally illustrated general coverage.

Gorenstein, Shirley. *Introduction to Archaeology*, 1965. New York: Basic Books. An especially lucid and pleasantly written book, which carefully introduces each stage of archaeological investigation and, at the same time, gives the reader some sense of the challenge and excitement inherent in much archaeological exploration.

Harris, Marvin. "What Goes Up, May Stay Up." *Natural History*, 1973, 72(1):18-25. A newer look at an old topic, the changes in women's fashions.

Heizer, Robert F. *The Archaeologist at Work*, 1959. New York: Harper & Row. A multifaceted collection of articles by researchers at work in all the various aspects of archaeology.

Heizer, Robert F. and John Graham. *A Guide to Field Methods in Archaeology*, rev. ed., 1967. Washington, DC: National Press. A thorough guide, well written and illustrated.

Kroeber, Alfred L. *Anthropology*, rev. ed., 1948. New York: Harcourt, Brace. Despite its age, an excellent basic text. Mentioned here for its material on culture history and research on women's fashions.

Kroeber, Alfred L. and Jane Richardson. "Three Centuries of Women's Dress Fashions." *Anthropological Records*, 1940, 5(2):i-iv, 111-153. A classic article on cultural change and women's fashions.

Mayer-Oaks, William J. *Prehistory of the Upper Ohio Valley*, 1955. Pittsburgh: Carnegie Museum. A study of discoveries in a United States Valley, noteworthy here as the source of the interesting chart illustrating the use of the seriation method on lighting devices.

Woodall, J. Ned. *An Introduction to Modern Archaeology*, 1972. Cambridge, MA: Schenkman. A concise, readable, and reasonable summary of some modern approaches to archaeology.

Project Nine

Analyzing
Folklore Content

Among the non-Western people traditionally studied by anthropologists, art is often a part of economic, political, and religious activities. Indeed, "the artist's work often represents symbolically the essence of the interrelationship between these basic aspects of culture" (Hammond 1971, p. 195). Verbal as well as graphic art is usually functional, although it may also be decorative or entertaining. For these reasons, anthropologists speak of "folklore" or "folk art," which is basically the lore, or the expressed learning, of the "folk," the people.

Many forms of aesthetic expression may be studied. There are the graphic and plastic arts: painting, sculpture, carving. There is instrumental and vocal music and the dance. Tattooing, personal adornment, and head-shrinking may also be considered folk arts in some cultures. But the aspect of folklore that has received by far the most attention from anthropologists has been oral literature. There are various categories of oral expression that have received particular emphasis.

Myths are generally defined as "traditionally based, dramatic narratives on themes that emphasize the nature of man's relationship to nature and to the supernatural" (Hammond, p. 318). Most students will be familiar with the myths of ancient Greece and Rome, which explained the origins of the world, the nature of the gods, and the foundations of the moral system of the world of human beings. We have come to use the word "myth" as a synonym for any story that is untrue, made up, or fanciful in some way. Yet, in the anthropological context, the scriptures of any living religion are myths in exactly the same way as are the stories of the no-longer-active religions of the ancients. The word "myth" should not be understood as a term of disparagement. Myths can refer to *any* stories that seek a transcendent explanation of *why* things got to be as they are, regardless of whether they can be verified or whether they are part of the structure of a living religious system.

On another level, we may also describe certain nonreligious tales as mythic because they explain people's relationship to the impersonal forces around them. A good example is the so-called mythic "Western," which draws on the concept of the frontier as being the breeding ground of a specific type of American personality. The mythic Western hero is the rugged individualist with a natural sense of justice, honor, and dignity of labor. Unemotional, the Western hero is forever a stranger riding off into the sunset and on to a new town. It is not important whether such people really existed, or were in any way statistically typical of the entire population. They are mythic because they are used, in numerous books, movies, and television tales, as symbols of the relationship between the rugged but bountiful land of the West and the pioneers who tamed the wilderness. In anthropological terms, such a figure is mythic because it expresses the highest aspirations of the culture.

Legends, in contrast to myths, provide a traditional moral sanction for action, and tend to be more concerned with *how* things got to be as they are. They may lack a supernatural basis, and are seldom as closely identified with the central belief system of a religion or ideology as are myths. Legends may be strictly local in nature, such as stories explaining how a particular deserted house in a certain town is "haunted" by the ghost of a tragic former inhabitant. But they may also be nationally known, as are the stories of Paul Bunyan, John Henry, and Johnny Appleseed.

The subject of a legend, like the subject of a myth, need not have been a real person, although the American tradition seems particularly rich in legends concerning real historical personages. In such cases, it becomes difficult to separate out the legendary from the historical aspects of those people: did Davy Crockett really kill a bear when he was only three? did George Washington really chop down the cherry tree? did Abraham Lincoln really walk twenty miles in the snow to return two cents to a grocery customer? Legends are recounted in much the same way as are fairy tales, although they lack the element of the supernatural common to the latter. The purpose of these often amusing or exciting narrative forms is largely instructional. They are entertaining little sermons on various values that the culture holds dear: courage in the face of impersonal power (John Henry), altruism (Johnny Appleseed), the pioneering spirit

(Paul Bunyan), honesty (Washington), integrity (Lincoln). They are used to teach children these values, and they are expressions of the adults' belief in the worth of these attributes.

It is interesting to note that some widespread legends reveal subtle shifts in both plot and structure in order to conform to local norms. For example, the familiar story of Jack and the Beanstalk is found in both England and the United States. The English version emphasizes giving and getting in a balanced, harmonious relationship. It focuses on the theme of a boy doing something noble to help a mother whom he has earlier made to suffer. In the American version, however, the dominant image, that of the sprouting beanstalk, is also the dominant theme, that of individual aspiration. The American story is very much concerned with showing off, and exhibiting male prowess (hunting, fighting), according to Martha Wolfenstein (1965), the scholar who compared the tales. The same story, told in different cultures, will reveal something about the way people in those cultures think about the world.

Proverbs may be thought of as shorthand versions of legends that in a sentence or two of witty or otherwise memorable expression present an example of "ethically approved behavior taken from the past or from other places" (Hammond 1971, p. 319). Proverbs may thus be used as moral guides, for instruction in approved values, and also for indirect social comment or criticism where more open expression would be inappropriate and/or dangerous.

Riddles, in most cultures, are used for entertainment purposes. In our society, they are considered a somewhat childish form of amusement; elsewhere they are used by adults to exercise their wit and their linguistic skill. Moreover,

> Their analysis can be useful to the anthropologist interested in acquiring insight into the characteristic patterning of a particular people's mental processes, the symbols that dominate their thought, the manner in which they categorize aspects of reality, and the patterned ways in which they perceive relationships (Hammond, p. 321).

Miscellaneous forms such as verbal abuse, games, nicknaming, toasts, and graffiti may also be said to be part of the folklore tradition. The student is directed to Maria Leach (1949-50) for other definitions and explanations of forms studied by folklorists.

Uses of Folklore Analysis

For the anthropologist, art, including folklore, is best understood in its cultural and social contexts. Consider, for example, limitations in technology that reduce the available methods of expression; cultural beliefs in what is valuable that direct the activities of artists toward certain types of expression; limitations in resources that restrict the materials that can be used, and so on.

The artistic product, therefore, is the result of a process both of interpersonal relationships and of relationships between people and their environment. But the product itself may be of great use in an anthropological study, particularly when it is not possible to do a detailed ethnographic analysis of the culture as a whole. One of the most interesting applications of this aspect of folklore analysis was initiated during World War II when it became necessary to understand the cultures of the people with whom we were at war, or with whom we were allied but could not visit due to wartime restrictions on travel. Since the war itself made firsthand fieldwork difficult or impossible in many areas, a group of anthropologists determined to study "culture at a distance" and, to that end, analyzed folklore and other manifestations of "popular culture" (magazines, films, books) in order to glean information about the Japanese, German, Russian, and many other cultures. In order to understand the rationale behind this approach, it is necessary to understand that the folk art product is a medium for learning and transmitting cultural information. If a legend, for example, passes on the knowledge of a value from one member of a society to another, then the analysis of that legend by anthropologists will enable them to learn which values are being upheld in that society, even if those conclusions cannot be verified with firsthand observation.

Like any product of expressive behavior, folk art may usefully be analyzed on two levels: in terms of its forms, and in terms of its content. Perhaps the most detailed formal analysis of any folk art has been done by Alan Lomax, who developed an elaborate typology of song structures, rhythmical patterns, rhyme schemes, and so on, and correlated them with specific types of social structure. In recent years, there has been an increasing concern with distributional studies of folklore types, in which the elements of the folklore product (particularly characters, types of openings and resolutions, sequences of events) are mapped to show how they have spread, and to determine which types of societies tend to be associated with which types of structure and/or plot motif.

Despite the importance of these formal studies, the analysis of the content of folklore has occupied most students in the field to date. The content of anything can be either manifest (obvious, explicit) or latent (hidden, implicit). The artist who creates a particular work of art may have a specific purpose in mind when forming a product, which will be the manifest content of the work. Yet since that artist is a member of a cultural tradition, the values, attitudes, and beliefs most commonly held by members of that society will naturally, and without deliberate attempt, find their way into the work. Moreover, the artist is an individual with particular attitudes, beliefs, and personal interests. As a result, the latent content of the work provides a text for the analyst, who may be able to see those aspects of the culture that are so taken for granted—or those aspects of the personality of the artist that are not specifically explained—that they turn up even when the artist is making no particular effort to include them.

These points may be illustrated with reference to one particular folk art form: the Trinidad calypso. In the form familiar in North America and Europe, calypso tends to be associated with a type of ditty with doggerel lyrics sung in a "quaint" island accent to the accompaniment of a peppy, danceable beat. But according to the Trinidadian novelist V. S. Naipaul:

> It is only in the calypso that the Trinidadian touches reality. The calypso is a purely local form. No song composed outside Trinidad is a calypso. The calypso deals with local incidents, local attitudes, and it does so in a local language. . . . Wit and verbal conceits are fundamental; without them no song, however good the music, however well sung, can be judged a calypso (1962, pp. 75-76).

According to the Trinidadian drama expert Errol Hill, calypso is a form of the "minstrel art," and he has made a detailed study of the history of the calypso as an independent art form. It is, therefore, appropriate to analyze the calypso to help understand the culture of the Trinidadians who produce it.

Calypso is most closely associated with Carnival, the riotous public theater that is the focus of Trinidad's social life. Each year just after Christmas, the several dozen professional calypsonians release a set of new calypsoes, songs of personal and social commentary, which are then sung all over the island the next two months. These performances culminate in Carnival, which occurs on the two days preceding Ash Wednesday, ushering in the penitential season of Lent. The calypsonian who is judged to have produced the best set of calypsoes for the season will be crowned

Calypso King. The individual song that is judged the best will be named the "Road March," and will be played by steel bands parading the streets during Carnival. Thus the calypso is not merely any old song; the composition, performance, and judging of calypsoes is a major activity in the lives of the people of the island.

Although Trinidad is a nation with a free press and a vigorous modern communications network, political and social commentary come alive in the singing of calypso. The government, public figures, events, and fashion trends are all fair game for the calypsonian — who has license to speak out in a way that not even the most daring newspaper editorialist would attempt. In one season, for example, the major topic of conversation was a recent, abortive army mutiny, which was being referred to as the "April Revolution." This event was followed by a strict curfew, the roundup of members of the political opposition, and a sensational military trial. These dramatic political events were discussed heatedly during the year, but only the calypsonians could risk going public with critical points of view.

Lord Kitchener, one of the greatest of the calypsonians, entitled his collection of songs for that season "Curfew Time," and so one might have said that the manifest content of his calypsoes was the new political climate. However, by analyzing some of the songs individually, it is possible to see the latent content, which says quite a lot about Trinidad society. The calypso "Curfew Time," for example, is not merely a criticism of government policy. It is also a series of amusing double entendres that leave no doubt in the listeners' minds that the singer used the order to stay home after dark for purposes other than discussing politics. One of the great traditional themes of calypso, reflecting a preoccupation of Trinidad life, is that of the sexual tug of war between men, who are eager to skip from conquest to conquest, and women, whom the men portray as inevitably surrendering to the superior male magnetism. This statement of an essential personal value thus comes into a calypso that has a superficially political purpose. The calypso "PP 99" is manifestly a comment on increasing government interference with private rights, in the form of meter maids who check on the revered island custom of illegal parking. But the resolution of the song suggests that Lord Kitchener believes that, if all else fails, he will thwart the meter maids by asserting his masculine sexual dominance over them. "Let Them Crow" is, overtly, a statement in which the calypsonian dares the government to cancel Carnival (an action that had been threatened because of fears of renewed outbreaks of violence in the wake of the "revolution"). Covertly, it is a statement of the fundamental Trinidadian belief that no "authority" can push a man around. "I go do what I damn please" is the motto.

From the analysis of the content of these calypsoes, it is possible to discern not only the manifest concern with the overriding political issues of the day, but also a continuing expression of certain values regarding the expected norms of sociosexual behavior.

In summary, we may say that folklore serves several social functions. The analysis of folklore by an anthropologist can tell us something about the social character of the people who create and use it.

> In addition to the obvious function of entertainment and amusement, folklore serves to sanction the established beliefs, attitudes and institutions, both sacred and secular, and it plays a vital role in education in non-literate societies. . . . But, in addition to its role in transmitting culture from one generation to another, and to providing ready rationalizations when beliefs and attitudes are called into question, folklore is used in some societies to apply social pressure to those who would deviate from accepted norms. . . . Beneath a good deal of humor lies a deeper meaning, and . . . folklore serves as a psychological escape from many repressions, not only sexual, which society imposes upon the individual (Bascom 1971, p. 474).

The Project

Although anthropological studies of folklore have tended to concentrate on the technologically primitive, small-scale societies that are the traditional foci of ethnography, it is both possible and desirable to study the folk output of societies such as our own. This task, however, is complicated by the heterogeneity of cultural traditions within American society and by a multilayered creative process which, according to Tristram Coffin and Hennig Cohen (1986), results in a threefold division of folklore products:

- the literary tradition
- the popular tradition
- the oral, or folk tradition

Since the United States is, generally speaking, a literate society, a large part of our common folk traditions, particularly in the verbal arts, is bound up in material that we have assimilated through the formal education process. Legends such as those of Moby Dick, the Celebrated Jumping Frog, Tom and Huck, or the courtship of Miles Standish have all entered our folk consciousness through some recognized literary sources. Even those who have never read Longfellow's poem, for example, will know the line, "speak for yourself, John," and will be able to tell the story of which it is a part.

At the other extreme are the oral traditions, which are made up of all the materials that people "who can't, don't, or won't write pass on from generation to generation by word of mouth" (Coffin and Cohen 1986, p. xiii). Because of the overwhelming influence of literate educational facilities in our society, our purely oral folk tradition is rapidly dwindling, but it still exists in isolated communities or in the form of a number of minor arts, such as proverbs and games. More fully articulated folk narratives (tales, legends, and so on) may still be found relatively intact among the many ethnic, religious, or occupational cultures within the larger U.S. society.

The vast middle ground, however, seems to support the bulk of contemporary American folklore. This popular tradition goes back at least as far as the ballads of Stephen Foster, with their self-conscious evocation of the plantation folk styles. To quote Coffin and Cohen:

> The songs of Stephen Foster, George Gershwin, and Bob Dylan which deliberately imitate folk music because it is profitable to do so; the calculated promotion of fictional figures like Pecos Bill . . . in order to provide the local color that attracts tourists; the transformation by script writers of Billy the Kid and Davy Crockett into television heroes to sell cereal; and even the more or less innocent fabrications of children's stories such as that of George Washington and the cherry tree, designed to teach reading and moral behavior — fall within the popular tradition (1986, p. xiv).

Although many of these products are consciously created by particular artists or entertainers and are not created by "the folk," they are often vigorous parts of the living folk tradition. For example, Woody Guthrie's Depression-era songs about the Dust Bowl and the labor unions are now treated as genuine folk expressions that are much more revealing of "folk" attitudes in a now-distant period than any number of objective history books. More recently, the theme song of the international famine relief project, "We Are the World," has achieved such general currency as a popular anthem that its authorship is immaterial — it is a song that satisfies a felt need and has been adopted as a popular statement, just as if it were actually a spontaneously unselfconscious "folk song."

The folklore analysis project will have two main aspects: the collection of a sample of folkloristic material, and the analysis of its content along the lines suggested above.

Procedure

I. Select one example representative of any one of the three main types of American folklore. Some suggestions:

  A. Literary Tradition (broadly interpreted)
1. Western novels by Zane Grey
2. epitaphs from old tombstones
3. an anthology of cartoons such as *Peanuts, The Far Side, Doonesbury,* or *Bloom County*
4. a series of episodes from any popular TV series that features a continuing set of characters
5. a collection of graffiti

  B. Popular Tradition
1. the work of a contemporary song composer, either one who is active in the student's local area and to whom the student has access, or a well-known recording artist
2. one particular work of such a composer (particularly a song with an extended narrative content); try not to rely on published analyses of such songs by professional music critics — choose one to which you can apply a fresh perspective without "contamination" from analyses by others

  C. Oral Tradition
1. narratives, legends, tales told by members of special ethnic or occupational groups
2. children's playground games
3. proverbs of an ethnic group
4. the "real" folk songs
5. jokes and riddles

The student is also directed to Clarke and Clarke (1963) for a more detailed survey of possible folklore topics that might readily be collected by the nonprofessional.

II. Make sure that you have full texts to work with. If you are dealing with songs, the lyrics should be available to people reading your report; you may use printed sheet music if available, or a transcript from a recorded performance. When collecting non-written material, such as proverbs, it is best to tape the informant who is reciting. For non-verbal activities, a series of photos would be helpful for a reader trying to follow your analysis.

III. Although the student will want to say a few words regarding the structure of a piece of folklore, the report should be geared toward an investigation of the content of the piece under analysis.

IV. For the piece of folklore you have chosen, write a brief summary consisting of answers to as many of the following questions as may be relevant: What is the piece of folklore you have chosen? Describe it. Describe the context in which it is typically found. Discuss how you collected it. Who else beside the performer was present? Under what circumstances? What was the atmosphere like (i.e., somber or happy, reverent or lighthearted)?

   A. What is the source of the material in both time and place? For example, a collection of Yiddish proverbs might be collected in New York City in 1991, but they are derived from Eastern Europe circa 1750. The question of provenience (the source of the material in time and place) also includes the question of influences: what (if any) sources outside the community in which this piece is performed influenced the adoption of this folk form? What (if any) other arts in other communities have been affected by this folk form?

   B. Is this piece of folklore typically the work of one individual artist or group of artists? If so, how is he or she (or are they) identified? If not, who also performs it? In what ways have the form and content changed by passing through other hands? If a song has a set of copyrighted lyrics, do other people who typically sing it change certain of the lyrics? If so, which ones? How? Why?

   C. What are the recurring motifs in this piece of folklore?
     1. verbal phrases
     2. physical activities of both the performer and the audience
     3. the style that is appropriate to the performance
     4. Is it mythic or legendary in any way? How? To what social goals (if any) is the myth or legend directed?

D. What are the recurring themes of the piece? Which values, attitudes, or behavior norms do they uphold? How? Is the piece used to teach these attitudes to children or others in the society? Which of these themes is manifest in the work? Which are latent? How can you account for the differences in latent and manifest content?

E. Are the expressed values, attitudes, or behavior norms typical of the group as a whole (in which case the artist is reflecting such norms), or is the artist trying to impose his or her values on the society?

The student is directed to Crowley (1983) for an example of this type of analysis applied to an extended set of folk narratives.

After completion of this analysis, three students who selected pieces representing the three different aspects of contemporary American folk art might want to make a joint presentation to discuss the differences in the three types, as well as the similarities, if any.

The continued outline below includes further suggestions with regard to gathering, reporting and analyzing your data.

V. When gathering data from a live informant

A. Be sure you have made observations and/or recordings on at least two occasions if at all possible, in order to verify that lyrics, actions, styles, and so on are really part of the work and not just temporary accidents.

B. As a general rule, older people are much better sources of information about folklore than young people, even when it comes to typical children's lore, such as fairy tales or games. But do not overlook the fact that children and adolescents have a folklore of their own, even if it is not rooted in many generations of tradition. Such behavior will be less obvious to the casual observer, but if the student is in prolonged contact with a group of young people, he or she may be able to get a clearer picture of their own particular folklore. One possible field of analysis in this context might be slang vocabulary, which has a very fast turnover rate.

VI. When reporting the data be sure that your sources of information are clearly indicated. Provide transcriptions of taped interviews, references to published sources, and photos of nonverbal behavior whenever relevant, and wherever feasible.

VII. When analyzing the data, remember that when dealing with the popular and oral traditions it will not always be possible to work with an extended *corpus* (body of materials). In the literary tradition, it is possible to say definitely that a certain collection of stories about the Old West represents the unified vision of a known author like Zane Grey. When working with the more diffuse forms, however, such as one song by a composer whose other work is unknown, it is unwise to strain after consistency or unifying themes. Nevertheless, because even these arts are, to one degree or another, socially conditioned, they will reveal certain themes and patterns that they have in common with other productions of the same culture. Even a nonunified collection of materials (political slogans painted on walls during an uprising) can be analyzed to show certain dominant social themes.

Selected Annotated Bibliography

Abrahams, Roger. "The Toast: A Neglected Form of Folk Narrative." In Horace P. Beck, ed., *Folklore in Action*, 1962. Washington, DC: The American Folklore Society. A leading contemporary folklorist discusses a minor but intriguing example of American folklore.

Barnouw, Victor. *Culture and Personality*, 4th ed., 1985. Homewood, IL: The Dorsey Press. Includes a good chapter on art and folklore as expressions of the personality of the individual artist, as well as mirrors of dominant social and cultural values.

Bascom, William R. "Folklore and Anthropology." In Lowell D. Holmes, ed., *Readings in General Anthropology*, 1971. New York: Ronald. A clear and concise abridgement of a longer article spelling out the uses of folklore analysis for the anthropologist.

Clarke, Kenneth W. and Mary W. Clarke. *Introducing Folklore*, 1963. New York: Holt, Rinehart and Winston. A basic manual that describes various folklore types, and provides some suggestions for the collection and analysis of such material.

Coffin, Tristram P. and Hennig Cohen. *Folklore in America*, 1986. Lanham, MD: University Press of America. An excellent, heterogeneous collection of folk productions in the United States.

Creighton, Helen. "Cape Breton Nicknames and Tales." In Horace P. Beck, ed., *Folklore in Action*, 1962. Washington, DC: The American Folklore Society. A lively discussion of a minor but interesting form of folklore as found in a distinctive local culture.

Crowley, Daniel J. *I Could Talk Old-Story Good: Creativity in Bahamian Folklore*, 1983. Berkeley: University of California Press. A sociocultural analysis of folk products; entertaining reading and a good model for the student's own analysis.

Dundes, Alan. "Structural Typologies in North American Indian Folktales." In Alan Dundes, ed., *The Study of Folklore*, 1965. Englewood Cliffs, NJ: Prentice-Hall. An example of formal and distributional analysis.

Edmonson, Munro. *Lore: An Introduction to the Science of Folklore and Literature*, 1971. New York: Holt, Rinehart and Winston. A highly regarded survey of the field of anthropology and folklore; tackles theoretical as well as methodological issues in the study of traditional literature.

Hammond, Peter B. *An Introduction to Cultural and Social Anthropology*, 1971. New York: Macmillan. Some good, basic information on the use of folklore analysis in anthropology.

Hill, Errol. *The Trinidad Carnival*, 1972. Austin: University of Texas Press. A scholarly and beautifully illustrated analysis of a folk art.

Leach, Maria, ed. *Standard Dictionary of Folklore, Mythology and Legend*, 2 vols., 1949-1950. New York: Funk and Wagnalls. A standard reference.

Lomax, Alan J. *Folk Song Style and Culture*, 1978. New Brunswick, NJ: Transaction. An exhaustive compendium of research in the field of song structure and related social structures.

Mead, Margaret and Rhoda Metraux. *The Study of Culture at a Distance*, 1953. Chicago: University of Chicago Press. The classic exposition of the uses of the popular arts in the study of other cultures.

Naipaul, V.S. *The Middle Passage*, 1989. New York: Random House. Naipaul's comments on calypso and Carnival are perhaps overly chauvinistic, but they are good examples of the influence of folklore on social values.

Ross, G. "Revolution on the Walls: Paris." *Nation*, 1968, 207: 84-85. Slogans painted on the walls during a student uprising are a clue to the values of the protesters.

Sutton-Smith, Brian. "The Folk Games of Children." In Tristram Coffin, ed., *Our Living Traditions: An Introduction to American Folklore*, 1968. New York: Basic Books. A summary of research into a form of non-literary folklore.

Wallace, A. F. C. "A Possible Technique for Recognizing Psychological Characteristics of the Ancient Maya from an Analysis of Their Art." *American Imago*, 1950, 7:239-258. A theoretical analysis of Mayan artistic products that aims to make inferences about the culture in which they were produced and about the personalities of the individuals who produced them.

Wolfenstein, Martha. "Jack and the Beanstalk: An American Version." In Alan Dundes, ed., *The Study of Folklore*, 1965. Englewood Cliffs, NJ: Prentice-Hall. This article originally appeared in a volume on childhood in contemporary societies.

Project Ten

Doing Ethnosemantic Research

A nthropological research involves both the collection and the interpretation of information. Ethnography, the process of collecting material in the field, should be based on the objective description of observed or recorded events. Yet such descriptions need to be classified and organized so that the reader can get a coherent view of the culture.

The sources of the most basic ethnographic data are our native informants. But many anthropologists feel that any conceptual framework that allows them to organize these data must reflect their own cross-cultural perspective. Such a perspective allows them to fit the data from one culture into a broader, more nearly global framework. Since the study of *phonetics* utilizes a set of internationally standardized symbols (the International Phonetic Alphabet) for recording all the many languages of the world, the type of ethnography that utilizes a similarly global framework for analyzing cultural data has been called the *etic* strategy for fieldwork.

On the other hand, there are anthropologists who believe that when we impose our own categories for classification we are being ethnocentric. These researchers feel that the organization of the data should derive from the views of the native informants themselves. In linguistics, the study of the contrastive distributions of sounds that can be used to signal changes in meaning to native speakers of the language is known as *phonemics*. By analogy, the "homemade model" treatment of other cultural data is known as the *emic* approach.

Emic and *etic* have, unfortunately, become slogans or catchwords in some quarters, rather than clear-cut concepts. The student should be aware that they are used differently by different theoreticians, although in one way or another they all refer to this linguistic model, and are ultimately based on the assumption that, since language is the most basic cultural institution, the models by which it is studied can also guide the study of other human institutions.

It may be noted that language is, in many ways, a distinctively human attribute. All animals can communicate with each other, and many of the higher primates have very elaborate call systems. Yet only humans have the capacity to use language, defined as a set of arbitrary sound symbols that can deal in abstractions, combine to create new symbols, and be strung together according to certain rules (grammar) to produce lengthy, meaningful utterances. Although non-human primates in experimental situations have been taught to use certain aspects of language that were once thought to be exclusively human, there is as yet no evidence that they do so in nature. We speak of the symbols of a language as being arbitrary because their meaning is bestowed on them by those who use them in communication. Thus while a chimpanzee or a gorilla may, under controlled conditions, be capable of learning some of the symbols of a given human language, the fact that it cannot create those symbols indicates that the chimp or gorilla communication system (even if we were willing to call it a language) is qualitatively different from ours.

Language is the aspect of culture that comes closest to being "predictable." Every language has certain logical rules (for pronunciation, for word formation, and for grammar) whose structure can be charted and classified. For these reasons, language is often taken as a model by which other cultural activities may be organized, since all of them must be conceptualized through the use of language. One important *emic* data-collection strategy is known as *ethnosemantics*, and it is explicitly based on the study of language as a model for the logic of all other aspects of human behavior.

Before proceeding to the project, it will be necessary to understand something of the background of ethnosemantic research. This strategy is most characteristically used by anthropologists who also have a strong interest in the specialized subfield of anthropological linguistics, but it can be used conveniently by fieldworkers with other interests, as long as they pay heed to a few basic concepts.

One major aspect of ethnosemantics is the proposition that different cultures, like different languages, have their own specific rules and logical structures. (According to many linguists, these differences are merely on the surface, for, at the deepest levels, all human languages share important structures. This consideration, however, is not immediately relevant to the performance of this project.) All languages meet the same basic need for communication, but this need is answered in hundreds of different ways by the various languages of the world. In the same way, any culture is, in part, an adaptive mechanism that helps people cope with the environments in which they find themselves; yet if "survival" is the goal of all societies, there are many different ways societies can go about the task. Since languages must have rules and patterns in order to be used efficiently as communicative "codes," it is possible for a native speaker of one language to learn to recognize the regularities of another and hence to learn to use that other language. Similarly, if different cultures were lacking in logical rules, then there could be no science of anthropology, since it would be impossible for a person born in one culture ever to find a way into another. Just as the linguist studies the rules by which the structure of a language is built up, so the ethnographer can study the units of culture and discover the ways in which these units fit together to form a coherent, more or less consistent scheme that makes sense to the people living within that culture.

In English, for example, when we say the word "kill" and contrast it to "gill," any native informant would say that the two utterances have quite different meanings. Since everything about these utterances is alike except for the initial consonant sounds, we can assume that the difference between those two sounds signals the change in the meaning of the whole utterance. "K" and "g" are therefore distinct sounds in English. We say that they are different *phonemes*. Now say the word "ski" and then the word "key." You can hear, if you listen carefully, that two distinct "k" sounds are produced. The "k" in "key" has a small but noticeable added puff of breath ("aspiration") that the "k" in "ski" lacks. Nevertheless, in English we do not think this distinction is meaningful. In fact, if we put the aspirated "k" in the other place and say "sk^{h}i," it would still mean the same thing to a native speaker, even though it would sound a little peculiar. Therefore, the two separate "k" sounds are considered to be part of a single phoneme, since they do not contrast with each other in the same meaningful way that "k" and "g" do. In Hindi, on the other hand, there is an important difference between consonants that are aspirated and those that are not, and this difference would signal a change in meaning in any word in which those consonants appear. In Hindi the word "k^{h}il" ("grain") is different from the word "kil" ("nail") so that the variation between "k^h" and "k" is meaningful. They are separate phonemes in Hindi. Since this is a regular practice, a native speaker of English must remember to make such distinctions when learning Hindi, although such distinctions can be skipped over when speaking English. (See Gleason 1961, Chapter 15.)

The same pattern holds true for other aspects of culture. One well-known example is that of color terms. We sometimes use the ROYGBIV device to help us remember the colors of the spectrum (red, orange, yellow, green, blue, indigo, violet). But there is nothing in nature (a rainbow, for instance) that enforces this categorization—it is a purely conventional division of what is, in nature, continuously graded light. Other languages have their own conventional terminologies, even though their speakers can all "see" the same colors in the strictly physical sense. Native speakers of Shona (a language of Central Africa) and of Bassa (a language of West Africa) divide the spectrum as follows:

ENGLISH	purple	blue	green	yellow	orange	red
SHONA	cips^{w}uka	citema	cicena		cips^{w}uka	
BASSA		hui		ziza		

(Gleason 1961, p. 4).

In short, each culture will establish its own rules for seeing the boundaries around categories; thus what one "knows" (the process of "cognition") is influenced by what one is taught to filter out of what comes in through one's senses (the process of "perception").

These culturally defined boundaries on our cognitive capacities are set by the criterion of relative importance. For example, Eskimos have no single word for "snow," but they have many different words for different kinds of snow. Though someone from a temperate climate would see only one thing, "snow," and it would scarcely matter if it were icy, wet, hard-packed, loose, drifting, or anything else, to the Eskimo, whose survival depends on being able to be very precise about such environmental conditions, the distinctions are of immense importance. Eskimos therefore "see" and designate differences that someone from another culture would not.

On the other hand, if an Eskimo who had lived his or her entire life in the Arctic paid a visit to a large city, he or she would be impressed by the many vehicles to be seen in the streets, all of which were metallic, had four wheels, and were driven by some unseen force within the body of the object. If this Eskimo were of a curious temperament, he or she might begin asking people, "What is that thing?" and be told, "It's a car." He or she might well come to the conclusion that "These things are all cars, and all cars are pretty much alike." However, for those who live in the city, cars are *not* all alike. Even those who are least car-conscious make all sorts of critical distinctions among them, having to do with size, shape, type of engine, type of accessories, country of manufacture, year of manufacture, use to which each is put, and so on. People do so because cars are important to their survival, just as snow is important to the Eskimo. Cars can even be assigned emotional, value-laden symbolism: driving a Rolls Royce is emphatically not "just the same" as driving a Hyundai.

What our hypothetical Eskimo failed to do was to dig deeper into the ways in which people in the city distinguish among their vehicles. The question was too broad; and, although important criteria were suggested, nothing had been learned about the equally important criteria that distinguish different cars within the larger category. The Eskimo would, therefore, be at a loss if he or she ever had to deal with any particular car. He or she might not, for example, be able to make the distinction between a taxi and a private car since, to an outsider's eyes, they "look alike." This situation would be analogous to one in which a person would be unable to learn a new language if he or she never learned to understand the contrasts among the phonemes of that language.

The problem, then, is to define the *semantic domain*—the boundaries of the meanings—for certain broadly applied terms. This is done by establishing a *paradigm*—a model of that aspect of the culture—by asking certain questions, beginning with the most general and proceeding to the most specific. In the case of our Eskimo and the cars, an informant might be asked, "I've been hearing the word 'car' a lot since I've been here. Tell me, what is a 'car'?" The informant might answer to the effect that a car is a four-wheeled vehicle powered by some sort of fuel that is burned inside the body of the vehicle. At this point, a basic question might be, "What types of cars are there?" One might also ask, "What are the different things a car has?" or "What are the different things a car does?" Since such questions may help establish the boundaries of categories, they are known as *structural* questions. Questions of similar type that establish the boundaries of abstract concepts (rather than of material items) would be known as *attribute* questions.

These criteria go beyond the bounds of a standard dictionary definition, and begin to clarify what a "car" means in the lives of people of a certain culture. The Eskimo ethnographer would then review with informants a variety of items, all of which are "cars" but some of which are different from others in the category, on the basis of the informants' own definition of "difference."

An example from the research of one of the authors may serve to illustrate the logic of ethnosemantics. The study concerned the ways in which mentally retarded adults adapt to life in the community after release from state institutions. It was necessary at the outset to clarify the meaning of "mental retardation," since that label covers a multitude of syndromes and is often used very inexactly. (It is not, for example, clearly defined even in state and federal legislation mandating training programs for such persons, so that it is sometimes difficult to decide who is and is not eligible for public assistance.) One way to define the domain of mental retardation would be to consult a textbook in this field for a definition generally acceptable to professionals. One formulation is found in the work of Evans (1983, pp. 15-22), who presents what is essentially a *medical* model, as it is based primarily on the criterion of cause. The general category "mental retardation" is divided at the first level in terms of *primary cause*: organic, sociogenic, and unknown. The first two of these categories are then subdivided in terms of particular organic or sociogenic factors that may account for the problem. The two organic categories, genetic and acquired physiological defects, are further subdivided down to two more levels of specificity. A chart can be drawn from Evans' discussion. (See Figure 10-1.)

In studying this chart, it is possible to define any of several dozen different conditions of which mental retardation is a symptom. It is possible to see how these conditions relate to each other, and how they relate back to the basic causes of retardation.

The staff members of community agencies, however, rarely had such an explicit medical model in mind. Instead, their principal criteria for distinguishing among types of mental retardation were behavioral — how did their clients act, and what kinds of programs and training would most benefit those clients? Although one informant told the researcher, "There's only one distinction that counts: will they do what you tell them, or will they 'act out'?" most informants had more elaborate schemes that could be elicited by careful questioning. Figure 10-2 is one such model, reasonably typical of those collected from informants in various agencies.

This model begins with a familiar division of the types of mental retardation (profound, severe, moderate, mild) as used in the field of special education. The primary distinction is based on relative capacity to function as an autonomous individual and as a member of society, rather than on the causes of the condition. The more

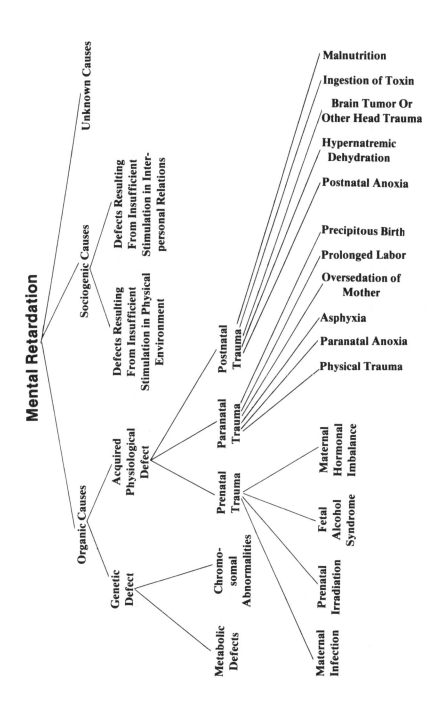

Mental Retardation

- Organic Causes
  - Genetic Defect
    - Metabolic Defects
    - Chromosomal Abnormalities
  - Acquired Physiological Defect
    - Prenatal Trauma
      - Maternal Infection
      - Prenatal Irradiation
      - Fetal Alcohol Syndrome
      - Maternal Hormonal Imbalance
    - Paranatal Trauma
      - Physical Trauma
      - Paranatal Anoxia
      - Asphyxia
      - Oversedation of Mother
      - Prolonged Labor
      - Precipitous Birth
    - Postnatal Trauma
      - Postnatal Anoxia
      - Hypernatremic Dehydration
      - Brain Tumor Or Other Head Trauma
      - Ingestion of Toxin
      - Malnutrition
- Sociogenic Causes
  - Defects Resulting From Insufficient Stimulation in Physical Environment
  - Defects Resulting From Insufficient Stimulation in Interpersonal Relations
- Unknown Causes

Mental Retardation

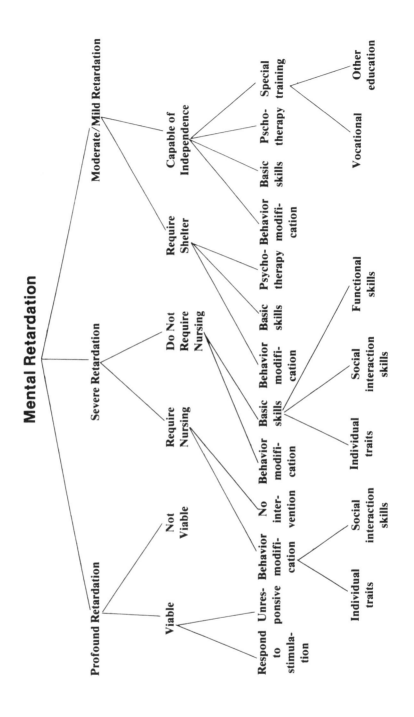

specific levels of the chart show how this informant categorized the kinds of intervention that could be used with clients in particular kinds of programs appropriate to their level of capacity to learn. For example, profoundly retarded people ordinarily have very serious physical impairments as well as mental retardation, and so are generally best cared for in an institutional setting. Some such people are "viable" (capable of living for years), while others are so impaired that their life expectancy is very short. Some of the viable profoundly retarded people respond to certain kinds of stimulation (physical contact, the sound of music), while others seem perpetually unaware of their surroundings. Similarly, some moderately or mildly retarded persons function quite well in sheltered workshops or supervised group homes, while others can learn specialized skills and, with the help of a variety of therapies, learn to live independently.

This paradigm was generated by asking questions of increasing specificity. It began with the very general query: "What are the different types of mental retardation?" At the next level, a typical question might be, "What kinds of profound mental retardation are there?" or "What kinds of severe mental retardation are there?" and so forth. This process could be followed until a level is reached at which the informant says, "There are no 'kinds' — that's all there is," as with unresponsive but viable profoundly retarded persons (for whom, therefore, no intervention is possible). The content of each elicited category could be determined by asking questions such as, "What is the most common reason for which a severely retarded person might need to be institutionalized?" (Answer: because he/she has medical problems that require a great deal of nursing supervision.) Then, "What are the things an institutionalized severely retarded person can do?" (Answer: some of them respond well to behavior modification techniques, while others don't; those who do can learn to modify their behavior on an individual level — not playing with their private parts, for example — and others can learn to modify their behaviors socially — learning to look directly at a person speaking to them, for example.) Such questions establish, in the first place, the *boundaries* of the semantic domain and, in the second place, the *attributes* of that domain. It is necessary to learn both things, or else the paradigm will be a meaningless list of words.

It is clear that the first model is useful to the physician attempting to *treat* a mentally retarded patient (or give counselling to expectant parents who happen to fall into a recognized group at risk). The second model is more useful to staff members at a school, workshop, or training facility whose aim is to help the client adjust as best he/she can to the demands of society. The two models are by no means mutually exclusive, but they do present different views of "reality" and represent different ways in which different classes of people—both professional experts—understand the problem of mental retardation.

Remember that any paradigm represents the *informant's* view of the world: it may or may not be the same categorization someone else would give. In fact, critics of the ethnosemantic approach, like Robbins Burling, have pointed out that the "logical possibilities" of classifying terms are so numerous that there might be no way to tell which of several possible models is the one that is "psychologically real" (1964, p. 26). It is for this reason that specialists or experts are so frequently chosen as informants, since their views will most closely approach the culturally accepted standard. Yet even experts can and do differ in their views of "reality." In our society, we could elicit the nomenclature of plants from a botanist and the result would be quite different from that elicited from a gardening hobbyist. Both are experts, but with different kinds of interest in the plants. In our society, science and the folk tradition are quite separate categories—one might almost say parts of separate cultures—although in most traditional societies the folk culture *is* the science. Ethnosemanticists working in traditional societies need not fear that the views of their expert informants will not be representative, although those working in our own society must necessarily be more explicit in defining those segments of the culture in which their informants are "experts."

When the paradigm is completed, the ethnographer will have a full model of the cognitive "map" of the informant and will, for example, understand all of the dimensions defining the domain "mental retardation." The ethnographer will then be able to tell the differences among people with mental retardation, even though not a professional specialist in the field.

One other means of generating a paradigm is to employ the method of "levels of contrast." For example, if we are interested in working out a classification of different types of animals, and we see a poodle and ask an informant, "Is it a plant?" "Is it a cat?" "Is it a collie?" we are eliciting information about three distinct levels of contrast. In the first case, the answer would be "No, it's an animal;" then, "No, it's a dog;" and finally, "No, it's a poodle." Therefore we have learned that there are at least three levels of discrimination for classifying this object:

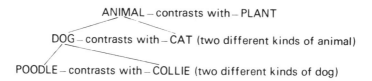

One must be particularly cautious in dealing with contrast-level types of questions because several words contrast at several different levels. In English, for example, the term "man" can have the somewhat general meaning of "human" in contrast to other kinds of animals (although the gender bias in the term has led most people to try to avoid using it in this context). At a more specific level, however, "man" contrasts with "woman" or "boy" or even one of several terms indicating an "unmanly" man. (See Frake 1961 for a more thorough discussion of these problems.) Remember, though, that even if the same word is used in a variety of contexts, there can be no category established as a semantic domain unless it contrasts with something else.

It is sometimes charged that the method of ethnosemantics is "too logical"—that people really never think about making such precise definitions unless they are prodded to do so by the inquisitive ethnographer. It is also likely that few nonbotanists, for example, really care why one thing is a "fruit" and something else is a "vegetable," as the important thing is to eat them, not analyze them. The point is that even though they may not make such careful distinctions as precisely or as frequently as the ethnographer might hope, they still maintain the cognitive structure typical of their culture, and everything that they experience is ultimately filtered through the "map" that unconsciously sets out the boundary markers of what they see or experience. Thus, by studying the cognitive structure in this way, one can learn a great deal about how people strive to make logical sense out of the welter of their perceptions.

Another criticism of the ethnosemantic method concerns its somewhat picayune nature. One may learn a lot about a plant, or a color, or a car by doing it, but is not such information trivial in the general scheme of things? And does it not take so long to elicit the paradigm of one minor aspect of a culture that we could never hope to use the method to study an entire culture? It is true that the ethnosemantic method would be quite tedious if every minute aspect of a culture were followed up in this detailed way. Yet despite this methodological drawback, the underlying theory remains sound. If one is convinced of the value of eliciting "homemade models" for understanding a culture, then ethnosemantics is a valid and highly informative way of going about it.

The Project

Select a semantic domain and create a paradigm for it. The first step is to select an informant with whom to work. Ideally, one might want to work with several informants in order to make sure that the answers one gets are truly representative. But many ethnosemantics specialists have gotten their results by working with only a single informant who also happened to be a specialist or expert in the chosen domain. For example, if one were interested in plants, a good informant might be a gardener. In some instances, a curer (herbalist, shaman, etc.) would also be familiar with many types of plants because he or she would use them in the act of curing. One could elicit from this person information on how to tell one plant from another. Plants might be distinguished on the basis of what they look like, what they are used for, where they grow, and so on.

You may wish to start with a relatively simple domain, one that you feel has only a few critical dimensions. For example, you might draw up a paradigm of the various types of burger concoctions served at a fast-food restaurant. If you are then feeling adventurous, or if you have some extra time, you may want to tackle something a bit more complex, such as interviewing a real estate agent about types of houses. You can use the real estate ads in the newspapers for clues as to what may be some of the critical dimensions of the category of "dwellings": size of rooms, number of rooms, location, type of ownership (private, cooperative, condominium).

If you speak another language, or have access to a bilingual informant, you may also want to try to compare the boundaries of domains cross-linguistically (and, by extension, cross-culturally) as in the color term chart on page 124. This latter approach can be tried as a team effort. One student may interview a French chef, another a cook who works in an Italian, or a Chinese, or a Mexican style. The domain might be cooking utensils. Even though Italian and Spanish are closely related languages, there is likely to be quite a difference in the categorization of utensils, reflecting the different roles of cookery in Italian and Mexican cultures. Although the several cooking traditions will each have unique features, certain criteria for establishing the domains will remain constant. For example, each one will have at least one thing used for stirring, as this is a motion required in virtually all styles of preparing food. It is, however, both interesting and important to see that in one tradition the stirring "thing" is metallic and rounded, while in another it will be wooden and flat.

The following example demonstrates regional variation in dealing with a category with which all people in our society are familiar: footwear. If you follow up on this example in your own area, you might well get some different responses and, hence, a different paradigm.

You may begin to interview your informant (a shoe salesperson) by asking a very general question, such as "What kinds of footwear do you sell in your store?" It is then important to check whether the answers are all at the same level of contrast. For example, the informant might say, "We sell dress shoes, sneakers, sandals, and deck shoes." However, upon further questioning you would learn that "dress shoes/sneakers" are not precisely a contrastive pair, because "dress shoes" is a very broad, general category, whereas "sneakers" is a specific case. Therefore, sneakers, sandals, and deck shoes are all examples of a broader category of "leisure shoes," which does form a contrastive pair with "dress shoes." You can therefore ask your informant to name various examples of dress shoes that would contrast, on their own level, with the specific examples of leisure shoes.

Next, you might want the informant to help you understand the criteria for distinguishing between dress and leisure shoes (what they look like, materials used in their creation, when and how they are used). You can do so with the more specific categories as well; thus, you would want to ask how to tell the difference between a "sneaker" (which, in some areas, means only that sort of lace-up canvas shoe with a ridged rubber sole and an extra pad of rubber covering the toes on top) and a "tennis shoe" (which can refer to lace-up canvas shoes that have flat rubber soles and no toe pad) within the larger category of "leisure wear." In preparing this project, we asked this question of numerous friends, both students and professional anthropologists, and got almost as many different answers as there were informants. People from certain regions of the United States make no distinction at all between "sneakers" and "tennis shoes," while others from different regions feel that "sneakers" are a variety of "tennis shoe," or vice versa. Others insisted that they were, in fact, distinct types, but, specified criteria other than the ones listed above for distinguishing between them. One might conclude, perhaps, that the example was not well chosen — it is such an unimportant part of our culture that people are very careless about using terms to describe it. Yet, in another sense, it is a highly illustrative example. In the first place, it indicates that something we take for granted as a known quantity (something too familiar to be careful about) is not nearly as "known" as we think. If people from the same culture (but having been brought up in different parts of the U.S.) can misunderstand each other and not recognize the alternative structures of meaning for a shared term, then imagine the problem in translating knowledge across a much wider cultural gap. The theory and method of ethnosemantics make us very much aware of how relative our knowledge can be. In the second place, the example illustrates the contention that the job of ethnosemantic researchers is to discover the meaningful criteria in the informant's terms, not in their own. The broader question of whether the information thus gained truly represents "everybody" has not yet been satisfactorily answered. The point here, however, is to use the method in order to elicit data, for without doing so, the question of representativeness can never be answered at all.

Your report should include a list of questions you used to establish your paradigm, as well as explanations for the terms within the paradigm.

Selected Annotated Bibliography

Basso, Keith H. *Western Apache Witchcraft*, 1969. Tucson: Anthropological Papers of the University of Arizona. An application of the ethnosemantic approach to a broad area of cultural behavior, rather than to specific, individual items.

Burling, Robbins. "Cognition and Componential Analysis: God's Truth or Hocus Pocus?" *American Anthropologist*, 1964, 66:20-28. A critical survey of the theory behind ethnosemantic research.

Conklin, Harold C. "Hanunoo Color Categories." *Southwestern Journal of Anthropology*, 1955, 11:339-344. One of the most widely cited ethnosemantic studies.

Evans, Daryl Paul. *The Lives of Mentally Retarded People*, 1983. Boulder, CO: Westview Press, 1983. Cited as a source of a professional definition (paradigm) of mental retardation.

Frake, Charles O. "Diagnosis of Disease among the Subanun of Mindanao." *American Anthropologist*, 1961, 63:113-132. Another pioneering ethnosemantic study; it deals with categories of disease, but contains some useful models for the creation of paradigms in other semantic domains.

Gleason, H.A. *An Introduction to Descriptive Linguistics*, 1961. New York: Holt, Rinehart and Winston. A standard textbook in linguistics that may be of some help to the student interested in learning some more about the background to ethnosemantic research.

Hockett, Charles F. "Chinese versus English: An Exploration of the Whorfian Theses." In Harry Hoijer, ed., *Language in Culture*. American Anthropological Association, Memoir No. 79, 1954. A brief, readable account of the cognitive differences between two language/culture systems.

Keesing, Roger M. "Paradigms Lost: The New Ethnography and the New Linguistics." *Southwestern Journal of Anthropology*, 1972, 28:299-332. A critical survey of research in the ethnosemantic tradition.

Patterson, Francine, and Eugene Linden. *The Education of Koko*, 1981. New York: Holt, Rinehart and Winston. A good introduction to the most famous of the experiments with teaching human language to a gorilla.

Spradley, James P. *The Ethnographic Interview*, 1979. New York: Holt, Rinehart and Winston. A clearly detailed how-to book by one of the most eminent practitioners of ethnosemantic research.

Spradley, James P. *Culture and Cognition: Rules, Maps and Plans*, 1987 (original 1972). Prospect Heights, IL: Waveland Press. A general survey of the status of cognitive anthropology; it is a much more sympathetic account than either the Burling or the Keesing article.

Spradley, James P. and David W. McCurdy. *The Cultural Experience: Ethnography in Complex Society*, 1988 (original 1972). Prospect Heights, IL: Waveland Press. A concise manual for doing ethnosemantic ethnography; also includes a collection of such ethnographies produced by undergraduate students. Students particularly interested in following up on this type of research will find this book a useful guide to some of the more refined techniques for establishing paradigms and dealing with other aspects of the general problems touched upon in this chapter.

Tyler, Stephen A., ed. *Cognitive Anthropology*, 1987 (original 1969). Prospect Heights, IL: Waveland Press. Another sympathetic survey of the field.

Wallace, Anthony F.C., and John Atkins. "The Meaning of Kinship Terms" *American Anthropologist*, 1960, 62:58-80. A widely discussed application of the paradigmatic model to the study of kinship terminology; kinship is one area of culture that seems to come close to language in being patterned into definite, cognitively defined structures.

Project Eleven

Designing a Survey

Surveys are among the most characteristic of social science data-collection techniques, although they are popularly associated with sociology or political science rather than with anthropology. In fact, surveys have been a part of anthropological research for a very long time — Lewis Henry Morgan's materials for his landmark volume *Systems of Consanguinity and Affinity of the Human Family*, published in the mid-19th century, were gathered from surveys, albeit of a cruder sort than those used today. A survey can be defined as a focused, organized means of data collection. As such, it is a logical and necessary complement to participant observation and related techniques based on subjective immersion in a cultural setting.

Surveys seem to answer a need for reasonably objective, quantifiable data, ours being a society in which "numbers" seem to impart validity to even the most general statement. Good survey research is, however, a more subtle process than simply asking a few questions and tallying the results. In his standard text on survey research methods, Babbie (1973, pp. 45-49) lists several criteria that distinguish *scientific* surveying from simply asking questions:

1. Survey research is *logical*. It yields results that can be objectively shown to be reasonable insofar as they can be quantified and described as clearcut patterns (e.g., if it is said that "75 percent of a representative sample of voters believe in the concept of public financing for presidential campaigns," then it would be impossible for anyone to argue, "But the people would really rather support only candidates of their own choice").

2. Survey research is *deterministic*. It is concerned with demonstrating linked associations between or among objectively defined events (e.g., to say that "55 percent of county health directors believe it is necessary for community health educators to possess the master's degree" means that there is a perceived link between academic training and job placement, a perception that is more than a plain, unfounded piece of intuition).

3. Survey research is *general*. The results should be applicable to a population larger than the specific group of respondents.

4. Survey research is *parsimonious*. Because a survey is a way of collecting and analyzing data on several variables simultaneously, it is possible for the researcher to construct a variety of explanatory models, and then select the one that most simply and adequately satisfies the hypothesis.

5. Survey research is *specific*. Although generalizable beyond the respondents, the survey is specific in that its units of measurement are clearly defined so that their relationship to each other can be presented objectively.

Furthermore, from the anthropological point of view, the development of a meaningful survey proceeds from the experience of participant observation. The researcher should ideally not formulate a questionnaire in isolation and hand it out to strangers. The anthropological approach is, as always, to try to be as much as possible a part of a community under study. The anthropologist's perception of the kinds of data that need to be gathered objectively by survey means should flow from first-hand experiences in the field.

Types of Surveys

Surveys serve three major functions of data collection. They can be used to *describe* the characteristics of a population, to *explain* the reasons for perceived associations between or among units, and to *explore* the extent of variables involved in a broadly defined issue as a prelude to a more focused study of the relationship between or among those units (Babbie 1973, pp. 57-59).

Surveys can be of two types. They can be *cross-sectional* in nature (describing, explaining, or exploring variables at one point in time), or they can be *longitudinal* (describing, explaining, or exploring changes in variables through time). There are three basic types of longitudinal survey: *trend* studies (based on descriptions of a general population, such as United States voters); *cohort* studies (focused on some specific sub-population, such as voters over the age of 50); and *panel* studies (based on the restudy of exactly the same respondents at different points in time) (Babbie 1973, pp. 64-65).

Sampling

It is conceivable that an anthropologist might work in a community small enough to permit interviewing everybody. For the most part, however, surveys are used when the community under study is too large to permit the researcher to contact each member individually. The researcher must therefore draw a *sample* to be surveyed. That sample must in one way or another be *representative* of the whole, or else the results of the survey cannot be used to say anything sensible about trends in the larger population.

The ideally representative sample is one in which all members of the total population have an equal chance of being selected as members of the sample. Such a group is called a *random sample*. The most common method of generating a sample has been *systematic sampling*, which means that, for example, every tenth name on an alphabetical list of students enrolled at a college, or every twentieth street address on a city census map will be selected. The starting point may be selected randomly, but then the system or pattern will be followed carefully. In such a procedure, the *sampling interval* is the selected standard distance between selected units (Babbie 1973, pp. 92-93).

An important modification of random sampling is the method of *stratified sampling*, in which a sample is not drawn from the total population, but from "homogeneous subsets" of that population. For example, a stratified sample of voters in a United States presidential election would be based on selecting numbers of each ethnic group, gender, social class, and so forth, numbers that approximate the percentages these groups represent in the total population. A simple random process, by contrast, might just by chance yield a sample that was 90 percent white and male, and such a group would not really be representative of current political opinion.

A further modification of the principle of stratification is *cluster sampling*. A researcher might want to survey a subpopulation whose general characteristics cannot be determined precisely enough to make stratified sampling possible. For example, it might be necessary to study "churchgoers in the United States." Clearly such a group cannot be determined easily, as nothing equivalent to a general census is taken of such persons. It is possible, however, to define "churchgoer" in terms of membership in several different types of denominations. Rosters of church members for those identified denominations can be obtained in a particular locality (assuming that the local area is somehow representative of national patterns) and then those members can be sampled (Babbie 1973, pp. 93-100).

The above methods are based on the science of *probability*; because the representativeness of the samples can be validated, statistical analysis can yield objectively defined association between and among variables. It is also possible, however, to draw *nonprobability* samples in situations in which precise representation is not feasible or necessary. One type of nonprobability sampling is known as *purposive* or *judgmental sampling*. For example, the researcher may select respondents who are considered experts in a given area. These experts need not be representative of the population as a whole (indeed, their special expertise means that they are not representative), but that defect is compensated for by the quality of their knowledgeable responses.

Although not usually a researcher's first choice, the *use of available subjects* may turn out to be the only kind of "sampling" possible at the time of the study, particularly if one is pressed for time. For example, the other students in your research methods class would be an easily available (and presumably cooperative) respondent group for your study. But one must be very careful and not make generalizations beyond such a non-representative group — their opinions or characteristics describe only themselves.

Formats

There are numerous surveys dealing with a variety of social issues that have been prepared, validated, and used repeatedly by professional researchers. Such *standardized surveys* have the very great advantage of allowing a researcher to use a ready-made instrument without lengthy developing and pretesting procedures. These surveys also permit the researcher to compare newly collected data with those collected with the same instrument but at a different time and place. A handy guide to available standardized survey instruments may be found in Miller (1983, pp. 271-568).

Because research problems differ from one site to another, and because different researchers have different foci for their projects, it is often not feasible to use a standardized survey. Hence a well-prepared researcher must be able to develop a survey instrument to meet the needs at hand.

Before one can even begin to design a questionnaire, one must answer some very basic questions of format:

1. Will the questionnaire be administered
   a. in face-to-face interviews,
   b. by telephone, or
   c. through the mail?
2. If "c" will the questionnaire be
   a. professionally printed,
   b. xeroxed or mimeographed, or
   c. faxed?
3. Will it require an explanatory cover letter?

Each of these apparently simple choices can make a real difference when one is planning a research project that must be kept to a strict budget and time frame. The pros and cons of different formats are reviewed by Williamson, Karp, and Dalphin (1982, pp. 141-144). No one technique is guaranteed to be ideal; each researcher must decide which format will yield the most benefits with the fewest possible drawbacks in that particular research setting.

Survey Construction: General Principles

As noted above, the design of a good survey involves more than simply listing all the questions to which one needs answers. All good survey research begins with careful background preparation. The available literature in one's problem area must be studied so that one can avoid asking questions that have already been settled, or can rephrase questions so as to shed new light on old assumptions. Studying the literature may also help the researcher understand what the current issues in a problem area really are.

In addition, anthropological surveys should ideally be developed only after the researcher has spent some time in the field, establishing rapport with members of the community, achieving a firsthand feeling for what the people believe the crucial issues to be, and acquiring a sensitivity for how they can most effectively be questioned about those issues.

It is always necessary to *pretest* a questionnaire before administering it to the respondents. The survey should be given to a small group to make sure that the questions are meaningful, clearly phrased, do not offend local sensitivities, and so forth. Appropriate modifications must be made before the survey is given to the selected sample.

With this background firmly in mind, the researcher should stop and ponder very seriously the question, "What do I need to know?" The ultimate answer should be boiled down to one or two basic themes. Unless one works for the United States Census Bureau, it is unwise to think in terms of a questionnaire that asks pages and pages of questions and deals with hundreds of variables. It is far preferable to limit surveys to a manageable size, lest the respondent grow bored or frustrated, and to limit it to just the several dimensions of one or two critical issues, lest the researcher get lost in the process of analysis. It is certainly possible to construct complex, compound surveys, and to analyze them with sophisticated computer-based statistical packages; but it is best to start learning what Williamson, Karp, and Dalphin call the "research craft" by working with narrowly focused instruments.

The first rule of good survey construction, then, should be to ask only questions that relate directly to the major issue that is to be investigated. As a correlate to that point, it is desirable to ask only questions that cannot be answered elsewhere. Do not, for example, ask respondents to estimate the number of people in their town if that information is easily obtained in standard references available in the public library. Researchers often include a block of "demographic questions" like age, sex, marital status, and educational level, because such items help in correlating responses later on. But it is well to be aware that such questions can be offensive to some people, and it is probably better to eliminate them if they are not absolutely vital to the main question.

A frequent problem in survey construction is one of specialization. Because researchers are so deeply immersed in their research problems, they assume that everyone knows the purposes of their surveys. In fact, this is not always the case, and researchers must take special pains to spell out their intentions in the clearest possible language. The careful definition of terms is sometimes referred to as *operationalizing the variables* so that it is always clear what is being asked. For example, if a researcher were interested in finding out how state directors of mental retardation programs distribute public funds to both institutional and community-based programs, he or she would need to be very careful to define precisely which programs are to be included in the rather hazily defined category "community service" *for the purposes of this study*. If such clarity is not provided, each respondent will answer the question in a way appropriate to his or her special circumstances, and the response will not be comparable to all the others.

It is wise to keep in mind the level of knowledge of respondents, especially if one's survey is to be used in support of some public policy. A typical "public opinion survey" asking "ordinary people" their opinions about arms control, for example, is certainly a valid index of current feelings; but it could not stand alone as a basis for formulating government policy — almost everyone will have an opinion on the broad issue, but few people will have sufficient detailed military, diplomatic, or political information to be able to say anything about the specific dimensions of policy. By the same token, the respondents' level of interest in the topic should be appreciated. A researcher may be vitally interested in learning what students think about types of endowed research institutions that might be established on campus, but since most students see such institutes as a very distant concern, they may answer only out of politeness and not give the questions very thoughtful attention.

One frequent mistake in survey construction is that of "overloading" the questions. Restricting a survey to just a few major variables has already been advocated; by no means should *one* question by itself deal with more than one variable. For example, to ask "What programs in social science are most helpful in preparing students for a career, and how do social science programs compare with programs in business administration?" is confusing to the respondent and may muddle the analysis. Programs in social science are one issue; programs in business administration are another; the student's perception of how they relate to one another is still a third.

Survey Construction: Response Modes

There are different ways in which questions can be asked, and the structuring of questions will have an impact on the way respondents cooperate in their answers. (See Orlich 1978, pp. 32-83 for a detailed discussion of the pros and cons of various response modes.) Decisions about response mode may be made according to the considerations discussed below.

1. Personal vs. Impersonal Style

The researcher may want to find out what the respondents feel to be true in a general sense. If so, the question might be, "Which courses of study in a college of public health are most useful to a student entering the field?'' However, that same question can be made more specific and personal: "What courses of study in a college of public health are most useful *to you* as a County Health Director?''

2. Item Sequencing

A good questionnaire is well-organized, and its questions flow logically from one to another. In certain standardized psychological tests, items are deliberately scrambled in order to measure how consistent the respondent's answers will be even in the absence of logical cues from the surveyor. In most cases, however, it is best to begin with the most general, least threatening kinds of questions and then build up to more complex or personal ones. Later questions should be based on information elicited earlier.

3. Forced vs. Open Response

Forced response questions are designed to use response categories that have been predetermined by the researcher (Orlich 1978, p. 43). The familiar multiple-choice exam is a special case of a forced-response mode. In designing a forced-response questionnaire, it is necessary to make sure that the choices listed are exhaustive, and yet not necessarily mutually exclusive. It is usually advisable to leave a final category, "other," to cover a choice that the researcher has not thought of. A mutually exclusive list (one on which the choices do not overlap) is more appropriate to opinion, rather than informational surveys. For example, a question might read:

"The college library is adequate for research needs of students."

    a. strongly agree

    b. agree

    c. undecided

    d. disagree

    e. strongly disagree

Such an "opinion" (or "attitude") question is answered on the basis of mutually exclusive forced-choice responses.

Open-ended questions, on the other hand, do not present the respondent with predetermined response categories. The respondent is free to answer the question in any manner that seems appropriate. For example, "How does the college library contribute to student research?" is an open-ended question. Open-ended questions should, however, be used only for items for which a forced-choice list cannot logically be constructed because open-ended questions can be difficult to analyze in a consistent manner.

4. Scales

There are three kinds of scales (systems of numerical notation) that are used with forced-choice questions.

> 1. *Nominal* scales (the response categories simply represent choices, those choices having no particular relationship to one another).

For example:

> A well-prepared community health educator will have a background in:
>
> a. epidemiology
> b. maternal and child health
> c. health policy and administration
> d. Infectious disease control
> e. other _____

The above is an example of a forced-choice response that is not a mutually exclusive list; two or more of the answers might be selected.

2. *Ordinal* scales (the response categories are rank-ordered with relation to each other). For example (asked of a staff member of a community mental retardation facility):

> When our budget for next year is developed, I expect to be working with:
>
> a. fewer clients than this year
> b. the same number of clients as this year
> c. more clients than this year

The above is an example of mathematical ranking. A non-mathematical ordinal scale might be one on which the items increase in perceived value:

> A county health director should have training at the following level:
>
> a. A.A.
> b. B.A./B.S.
> c. M.A./M.S.
> d. M.P.H./M.S.P.H.
> e. Ph.D./Ed.D./D.P.H.
> f. M.D.
> g. other _____

One widely used ordinal scale is known as a *Likert Scale* in honor of the researcher who developed it. The "agree-disagree" continuum used as an example above is the most familiar type of Likert scale, but there are other types of categories such a response mode can cover. For example (asked of a staff member at a community mental retardation facility):

The Board of Directors of this program is:

a. very supportive of our program staff
b. supportive of our program staff
c. unsupportive of our program staff
d. very unsupportive of our program staff

3. *Interval* scales (response categories are ranked in terms of *equal* differences between categories). For example:

The ideal size of a community mental retardation facility is:

a. 1-3 clients
b. 4-6 clients
c. 7-9 clients
d. 10-12 clients

5. Coding

Popular folk wisdom aside, "the facts" do not speak for themselves. It is necessary to convert survey responses into quantifiable form in order to make analytical sense of them. The process of converting raw responses into quantifiable form is known as *coding* the data. The researcher is responsible for assigning a numerical score for each response category on the forced-choice survey, and these codes appear directly on the questionnaire.

Nominal data are assigned codes arbitrarily, but systematically. For example,

After graduation, I plan to go into a professional career:
(1) yes
(2) no
(3) undecided

Such a code does not imply that "yes" is *less* than "no," but simply that the two responses are different and are given different reference labels. The data can be analyzed by counting the responses to every category (1), every category (2), and so on.

Because ordinal data do have a numerical relationship with each other, the coding needs to be assigned with great consistency. For example, in the number-of-clients question above, *all* questions in the survey that use this format should be coded in the same way. So, for example, *all* "fewer" responses would be coded "1", all "same" responses "2" and all "more" responses "3". The same consistency applies very definitely to the coding of Likert scale items.

Open-ended questions usually cannot be precoded, since it is impossible to predict the patterns of response; but such data must still be coded before any analysis can proceed. The researcher is responsible for discovering patterns in the narrative responses, inventing categories that seem to cover most cases, then assigning numerical codes. This is a tedious and time-consuming process, a good reason to avoid a multiplicity of open-ended questions. A good survey should not be entirely a "fishing expedition." (For a good, basic discussion on electronic data processing to supplement the guidelines for manual coding, see Orlich 1978, pp. 73-83.)

6. Protection of Human Subjects

Researchers are advised to familiarize themselves with current legislation regarding the use of human subjects. Your own university will probably have a set of published regulations that you can follow. Surveys generally fall outside the category of putting people directly at risk, although the possibility certainly exists for invasion of privacy. As such, appropriate steps need to be taken in order to insure the privacy of the data. For example, respondents' names should not appear on the response sheet and should be kept in coded form in the records of the researcher. The researcher might also include a cover letter pledging not to reveal any responses except in aggregate form (see the section on data analysis below) and to insure complete anonymity for all subjects. Subjects who are still uncertain that their privacy will be protected should not be pressured to participate. It is almost always desirable to ask respondents to sign a form indicating that the purposes of the research project have been explained to them, and that they are participating voluntarily in the research. Students may wish to familiarize themselves with the current *Statement on Ethics: Principles of Professional Responsibility* promulgated by the American Anthropological Association. A copy of this statement is reprinted as an appendix in Rynkiewich and Spradley (1981, pp. 183-186).

Data Analysis

Survey research exists in order to identify trends from data collected in a given sample. The craft of categorizing data for interpretation is known as *data analysis*. There are two basic ways to conduct data analysis.

1. Descriptive Analysis

The most basic act of "describing" data is a simple count of the number of responses per category. This procedure is known as a *frequency distribution*. Such distributions can also be usefully converted into percentages (e.g., "17 respondents, or 65 percent of the sample, indicated that they expect to be working with more clients next year than in the current fiscal year"). Basic descriptive statistical measures (mean, median, mode, standard deviation) are useful when presenting data, so as to give the reader a better idea of the overall shape of the distribution of responses.

2. Inferential Statistical Analysis

If a sample is drawn from a randomly distributed population, then the resulting analysis is called *parametric* statistics. When the sample is not randomized, analysis is based on *nonparametric* statistics. Nonparametric statistical tests establish relationships among variables, and involve such standard tests as the binomial, chi-square, and rank order coefficient of correlation (rho). The student is directed to Thomas (1976) for an introduction to statistical analysis written for the anthropologist.

The Project

Design, pretest, administer, and analyze a brief questionnaire on a topic of your own choosing.

1. Select a problem area in which you are particularly interested. It might be a good idea to select an issue related to something you are working on for another project, since you will then have done some background reading, and will have established some rapport in the community.

2. Boil your inquiry down to one or two basic issues. What, exactly, do you want to know? It is probably better at this stage

to choose either an informational survey (asking factual questions) *or* an attitudinal survey (asking opinion questions) rather than one that combines both.

3. Decide on a method of sampling, and select a format and response mode that you feel is most appropriate for your population.

4. Design your questions, keeping in mind the principles of construction outlined in the presentation of this project.

5. Pretest the questionnaire. The other students in your class, who are working on their own surveys at the same time, might be a useful pretest group.

6. Modify your survey if necessary. Make sure that you have precoded all forced-choice responses.

7. Administer your survey. Be sure to give yourself enough time to complete the project if you are mailing the survey to respondents.

8. Analyze the data. Present the results both descriptively and in terms of relevant inferential measures. Consult one of the suggested statistical texts to decide which tests would be most appropriate to your particular data, and to the particular aims of your project. In addition to the statistical analysis, your final report should include a statement about your research problem (relevant issues drawn from the literature), a justification for your sampling methods and general research design, and a discussion of the procedures taken to protect your respondents' privacy.

Selected Annotated Bibliography

Babbie, Earl R. *Survey Research Methods*, 1973. Belmont, CA: Wadsworth. The standard text in this field.

Blalock, Hubert M. *An Introduction to Social Research*, 2nd ed., 1982. Englewood Cliffs, NJ: Prentice-Hall. A concise overview of the field.

Brim, John A. and David H. Spain. *Research Design in Anthropology: Paradigms and Pragmatics in the Testing of Hypotheses*, 1982. New York: Irvington. An excellent review of "focused" anthropological research techniques (as distinct from broadly descriptive ethnographies).

Brown, Foster Lloyd, Jimmy R. Amos, and Oscar G. Mink. *Statistical Concepts: A Basic Program*, 2nd ed., 1975. New York: Harper & Row. A concise overview of the field.

Miller, Delbert C. *Handbook of Research Design and Social Measurement*, 4th ed., 1983. New York: Longman. A useful compendium of the principles of social research, mentioned here specifically for its extensive review of standardized surveys.

Morgan, Lewis Henry. *Systems of Consanguinity and Affinity of the Human Family*, 1870. Washington, DC: Smithsonian Institution. Included here as an early example of the use of survey techniques in anthropological research.

Murphy, Michael Dean and Agneta Johannsen. "Ethical Obligations and Federal Regulations in Ethnographic Research and Anthropological Education." *Human Organization*, 1990, 49: 127-135. An interesting object lesson in the ethical dilemmas of conducting a student research project in the context of current concerns about the protection of human subjects.

Orlich, Donald C. *Designing Sensible Surveys*, 1978. Pleasantville, NY: Redgrave. An easy-to-read presentation of the processes involved in survey research; uses examples drawn from educational research.

Rynkiewich, Michael A. and James P. Spradley. *Ethics and Anthropology: Dilemmas in Fieldwork*, 1981. Melbourne, FL: Krieger. A useful sourcebook in professional ethics, noted here especially because it contains the current American Anthropological Association ethical guidelines.

Thomas, David H. *Refiguring Anthropology: First Principles of Probability and Statistics*, 1986 (original 1976). Prospect Heights, IL: Waveland Press. A witty and helpful survey of statistical procedures, using anthropological examples and written for the student with minimal prior statistical training.

Williamson, John B., David A. Karp, and John R. Dalphin. *The Research Craft: An Introduction to Social Science Methods*, 2nd ed., 1982. Glenview, IL: Scott, Foresman. A thorough, well-written study of the larger context of social research, of which survey research is but one aspect.

Project Twelve

Studying Formal Organizations

Sociologists have been more inclined than anthropologists to study formal aspects of social structure, such as bureaucracies and corporations. Yet anthropologists have also recognized the utility of such investigations. Organizations, of course, do not always have written bylaws; more often than not, those studied traditionally by anthropologists are based on ties of kinship and ritual rather than statute.

Studies of African kingdoms by British anthropologists, for example, have shown quite clearly that elaborate bureaucracies can exist even in nonliterate societies (Fortes and Evans-Pritchard 1940). Similarly, a traditional, religiously oriented collection of people such as an Indian caste can be viewed as if it were analogous to a "corporate" structure in the West (Cohn 1971, Chapter 11).

Anthropologists try to apply consistent methods for studying formal organizations. One way they do so is to concentrate on the concepts of *status* and *role*.

In everyday English, the term *status* often implies prestige or rank, as when we say "That rich family has lots of status in our town." According to the social science definition, however, status is not necessarily defined hierarchically. A status is "a collection of rights and duties" (Linton 1936, p. 113). In other words, to say that a person is a "teacher" is to refer to one cluster of rights and duties that defines that position in relation to other individuals. Being a teacher, then, means occupying a particular status. Members of a society will occupy many statuses over the course of their lifetimes and will, in fact, occupy many of them simultaneously. A person is not only

150

someone's teacher, but also someone else's child, or perhaps someone's spouse. In addition, that person may be a union member, church member, volunteer firefighter, and so on. We may be born into some of these categories (*ascribed status*) such as one's sex, race or ethnic group. We may fit into other groups later in life on the basis of merit or attainments (*achieved status*). Our place in society is therefore the sum total of all the statuses we occupy. To be sure, many statuses are ranked: the status of school principal is higher than that of teacher; being a parent carries more authority than being a child, and so forth. However, this ranking need not be rigid. An individual who ranks high in one interaction (as a principal in relation to the teachers on the staff) will be subservient in another situation (as a member of a church congregation who defers to the minister).

> The relation between any individual and any status he holds is somewhat like that between the driver of an automobile and the driver's place in the machine. The driver's seat with its steering wheel, accelerator, and other controls is a constant with ever-present potentialities for action and control, while the driver may be any member of the family and may exercise these potentialities very well or very badly (Linton 1936, p. 113).

A study of the statuses involved in any institutionalized social situation can yield much valuable information about the way in which a community is organized. The anthropologist, however, is often concerned not only with the formal, ideal structural framework, but with the real behaviors that people exhibit. The behaviors associated with status are known as *roles*. "When [an individual] puts the rights and duties which constitute the status into effect, he is performing a role" (Linton 1936, p. 114). In many ways, role behavior is patterned and formalized, as every society will have certain approved ways of acting in any given situation. Yet, just as a performer has some leeway in interpreting a role in a play, so individuals in any society have a certain amount of freedom in acting out the several roles that are characteristic of their statuses.

There are certain things that we, in our society, think of as being appropriate parental behavior, and we tend to criticize any person who deviates outrageously from those norms. Yet within the range of acceptable parental behavior, there may be as many permissible variants as there are individuals in any given sample. For these reasons, anthropologists study status in order to discover how interpersonal relationships are structured in a society; they study roles in order to understand the ongoing dynamics of social interaction. The ideal and the real activities of people can then be compared from one society to another in order to better understand the cultural process. Culture, it should be remembered, is not a machine that rigidly molds all its members into one pattern of conformity. Culture may limit activity in some ways, but since it is a growing, changing, open-ended system of behaviors and attitudes, it must always allow for variability.

It is clear that the organization of statuses and roles will vary from one society to another. There may be a great concentration of statuses in some societies. For example, in a small hunting and gathering band, the same man who is your mother's brother is also your father-in-law and may also be a shaman who cures your illness, the leader of the hunting party that secures your food, the headman who leads you on a raid against enemies, the artisan who fashions your arrows, and so forth. In modern societies, on the other hand, it would be very rare for one's spouse, doctor, lawyer, senator, minister, teacher, and boss to be the same person. Clearly then, understanding the organization of status can tell us a great deal about the qualitative aspects of life in a society. Interpersonal relationships in other societies may actually be more complex than those in our own society because there are so many levels on which two individuals may be interacting with each other. In our society, such interactions are more nearly individualized.

Statuses must be paired in order to be meaningful. Such a pairing is known as a *dyadic* relationship. For example, the status of "teacher" is meaningless without the corresponding status of "student." The personnel of the various dyads may shift, as in the case of an elementary school teacher who also attends class as a student at a university. That one person, then, is a member of two different dyadic relationships with two or more different individuals. Yet on the structural, more abstract, level, the relationships are the same; they are both teacher/student dyads. We can then discuss the abstract dyad of teacher/student in studying a culture, and do so independently of the people we happen to observe in that relationship at a particular point in time. An ethnographer in the field would observe the many different real examples of this abstract dyad in order to see what sorts of role behaviors fall into the acceptable range of variation, and which are unacceptable. In the latter case, we could also attempt to discern *why* the observed behaviors are not acceptable.

The learning of statuses and roles by members of a community is part of the process of *socialization* or *enculturation*. Most discussions of this process deal with child development, but it is also possible to discuss socialization or enculturation with regard to adults. Every time individuals in any culture enter into new social situations, they must be socialized, they must learn what their new statuses entail, and what sorts of role behaviors are to be associated with them. In many cultures, certain highly significant changes in status are marked by *rites of passage*, elaborate rituals that mark a public confirmation of the fact that an individual has undertaken a new set of relationships. In our society we do not necessarily hold public feasts when we take new jobs, but there is a socialization involved all the same. It is somewhat difficult to study the socialization of any individual into an informal dyadic relationship: the question of how one initiates a new friendship, for example, has been studied very little by social scientists. Yet when we deal with formal organizations in which the process is made explicit (even if it is not commonly thought of as a socialization process like the one children undergo), we can get a much better understanding of how members of a particular society conceptualize ideal relationships, how they define "proper" behavior, and what leeway they are permitted in working out relationships.

Whether one chooses to do fieldwork in another culture or in our own society, the study of organizations can be of value in aiding the understanding of the ways in which individuals fit into larger units. We can use the following basic criteria for delineating a "formal" organization for the purposes of this project:

- it must be a group that transcends its individual members (that is, it must be something that will have some continuity regardless of changes in personnel)
- it must have a system of defined statuses recognized at least by the members of the group, and possibly also by outsiders
- it must have some way to sanction behavior — either by rewarding conformity to accepted behavior, or by punishing deviance from it
- it must have a regularized means of initiating new members into the group, and conveying to them their new place and the behaviors that will be expected of them.

An institution, or formal organization, may be studied in the following dimensions (derived from the work of the anthropologist Bronislaw Malinowski [1944]):

1. *Charter*: the set of stated purposes that define the values that the organization proposes to uphold
2. *Personnel*: the people involved in an institution as defined by their *statuses* within the organization; it is necessary to study how people are:

    a. *recruited* into these statuses and

    b. *socialized*, or trained to think in reasonable conformity with the organization's charter

3. *Norms*: the expected *role* behaviors of people involved in an institution

4. *Material apparatus*: the things people need in order to carry out their designated tasks within the organization

5. *Activities*: what people are actually observed to do, as opposed to what they are ideally expected to do

6. *Function*: the way in which the institution satisfies larger needs defined by the culture of which it is a part, and also the way the institution may create new needs of its own to which the larger culture must respond; this aspect of the institution is often referred to as the "corporate culture" in contemporary studies of business organizations.

The Project

One formal organization in our own society with which all students are familiar — but which is probably not often thought of as an object of anthropological study — is the college or university. Most postsecondary institutions in the United States are accredited by regional councils; accreditation is the formal authorization for the institution to grant degrees. These councils periodically review the activities of colleges and universities. This process typically requires a school to prepare a "self-study" which includes the compilation of quantified data (e.g., enrollment patterns, admission scores, degrees awarded) and the collection of qualitative data about the goals, attitudes, and values of students, faculty, staff, and alumni. This latter aspect of the self-study is very much like an ethnography of a formal institution. It may be useful, in fact, to prepare that self-study document in the terms suggested by Malinowski for the study of institutions from an anthropological perspective.

Every university, for example, will have a defined charter. Public universities created by state legislatures will be described in legislation that defines their purpose, scope, and goals. Those founded under private auspices will have similar statements written into documents that establish a board of trustees or an endowment foundation. Many institutions boil this complex mass of statutory documentation into what is often called a "mission statement," which is supposed to be the most succinct possible statement of the aims of the university, the particular values it seeks to promote, and the means it proposes to express those values and achieve those ends. The mission statement of the University of South Florida reads as follows:

> As the state's first metropolitan university, a prototype of the university of the future, the University of South Florida has sought from its beginning to apply the talents of its scholars and students to the problems facing modern society. The University's stated mission is "to achieve preeminence as a general purpose university of academic excellence." Its role as a five-campus comprehensive research university places particular emphasis upon the instructional, research and service needs of a major metropolitan region and an increasingly urbanized state and nation. In addition, USF has mounted a major campaign to achieve national recognition as an innovative educational center for intellectual, economic and cultural development that enriches the quality of life for all.

> The University of South Florida is committed to the goal of becoming one of the top 25 state-assisted universities in the United States by the year 2001.

The fact that this statement is couched in lofty and abstract terms is not unusual, nor should it be disturbing — in and of itself. It is not proof that academic institutions are not in touch with the real world. No "Charter" statement can be very specific — it is a statement of principles, not a concrete blueprint for action. It is therefore necessary to examine the other aspects that make an organization a living thing. Every university will have a formal organizational chart (a campus hierarchy) that diagrams the relationships among the constituent parts of the campus community and that specifies the statuses underlying those relationships. Having people in the right place at the right time is, after all, the first step in moving from abstract goals to definite action. The organizational chart of the University of South Florida runs to several pages. Only that small segment pertaining to student services is presented below as an example of how such a diagram might look.

Ethnographic methods (observation, interviews with key informants, and other data collection techniques discussed in this book) can be used to find out about personnel — how people are brought into this organization (what are the hiring practices?) and how they come to be made parts of the institution (what services are available that provide support for staff and students?). Consulting the personnel manuals, student catalogs, faculty union

Figure 12-1

**Organization of Student Services at
The University of South Florida**

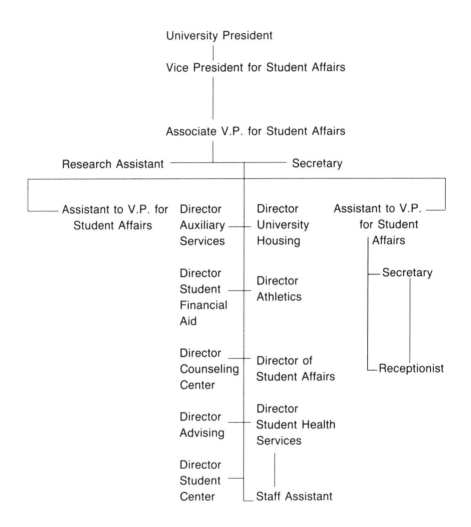

Vertical lines denote delegation of responsibility; those at higher levels supervise those at lower levels. Horizontal lines denote regular communication between those of equivalent rank.

contract, and other such documents will establish the boundaries of expected role behaviors associated with the labels on the organizational chart; these boundaries will establish the organization's *norms*. Such documents are normally open to the public. It is therefore possible to do an in-depth observation and interview and come up with case studies of particular people representing certain statuses to see how they actually go about doing the things they are supposed to do—how, in other words, do they define their *activities*? To what extent do they adhere to "guidelines?" To what extent do they modify those guidelines? How do they rationalize such choices?

It is also possible to do a material inventory of the environment of work and study on the campus—the *apparatus* of the institution. In a full-scale self-study, this aspect of the report can run to hundreds of pages of very detailed inventory, but it is possible, on a more limited basis, to determine what *kinds* of things serve the needs of the campus community (as opposed to the specific items currently in the inventory). What, for example, do you find in a typical professor's office? How is it the same as, and how is it different from, the office of a dean or vice president? How is a standard classroom (or laboratory, or student lounge) furnished? What kinds of spaces are there (seminar rooms, auditoriums, etc.)?

Finally, you might talk to leaders in the civic or professional communities served by the university—do they think students are well prepared? Do they feel welcome at the social and cultural events held on campus? In other words, how well does the institution match up with what the larger society expects a university to do? Conversely, have there been particular initiatives on the part of the university that have challenged the society and required them to rethink certain basic issues? In recent years, for example, centers for the study of values and ethics have been established on many campuses. These centers bring the traditions of scholarship to bear on ethical issues of current civic concern.

For this project, study your own university as a formal organization, following the outline detailed above. It might be most appropriate to do this project as a group—one student might study public documents, another conduct interviews, another do observations, and so on. If your university is a very large one, you might want to restrict the task to a smaller component—an academic department, the athletic department, the student housing bureau, or some such unit.

If it is, for some reason, not desirable or feasible to study your own campus, then each student might select an off-campus formal organization such as a civic club or political party for individual study. The organization should be large enough to allow the student to do a variety of data collection tasks, but not so large as to make it impossible to draw any conclusions within the time frame of a class project.

Selected Annotated Bibliography

Cohn, Bernard S. *India: The Social Anthropology of a Civilization,* 1971. Englewood Cliffs, NJ: Prentice-Hall. A concise ethnography, cited here because of its discussion of the corporate organization of the Indian family and caste system.

Fortes, Meyer and E.E. Evans-Pritchard, eds. *African Political Systems,* 1940. London: Oxford University Press for the International African Institute. A classic work of British social anthropology, cited here for its comparative discussion of political bureaucracies in non-Western cultures.

Frost, Peter, et al., eds. *Organizational Culture,* 1985. Newbury Park, CA: Sage Publications. A good casebook of studies, many of them ethnographic in nature, of formal institutions in modern societies.

Linton, Ralph. *The Study of Man,* 1936. Norwalk, CT: Appleton-Century. Contains what is generally regarded as the classic statement of the anthropological concepts of status and role.

Malinowski, Bronislaw. *A Scientific Theory of Culture,* 1944. Chapel Hill: University of North Carolina Press. A classic framework for the study of formal institutions.

Nespor, Jan. "Strategies of Discourse and Knowledge Use in the Practice of Bureaucratic Research." *Human Organization,* 1989, 48(4):325-332. An example of conducting ethnographic fieldwork in a modern bureaucracy; includes a theoretical discussion of the structure of communication within a bureaucratic organization, as well as some interesting comments on the adaptations needed by anthropologists doing fieldwork in such settings.

Parsons, Talcott and Gerald Platt. *The American University,* 1973. Cambridge, MA: Harvard University Press. A comprehensive sociological study of the university as a society and as a community composed of interlocking institutions.

Schein, Edgar H. *Organizational Culture and Leadership: A Dynamic View,* 1985. San Francisco: Jossey-Bass. A widely cited modern statement on the uses of the culture concept in the study of contemporary bureaucracies.

Project Thirteen

Taking Photographs

No matter what one's mental image of the modern anthropological fieldworker might be, we expect to see a camera — perhaps even a video camera — hanging somewhere on the person of the anthropologist busily doing his or her "thing."

Louis Daguerre perfected the first light-sensitive plate in 1837, and his daguerreotypes introduced photography to the world. Even in the earliest periods of photography, when the subjects had their heads held by vises and had to remain achingly immobile for long spaces of time, more than 95 percent of all daguerreotypes made in the United States were portraits of individuals, couples, or groups (Rudisill 1971, p. 198). Early writings about photography stress that photographs can confer a form of immortality, and a sitter can be held forever before a loving eye. Throughout the history of photography, then, it is not only anthropologists who have felt that "the proper study of mankind is man." The timeless appeal of pictures of people is well illustrated by popular collections such as *The Family of Man* (1955), once a travelling exhibition and now a much-reprinted book, and by the liberally illustrated book *Family* (1965), which combines the anthropological talents of Margaret Mead with the superb photography of Ken Heyman.

At one time, only occasional enterprising anthropological fieldworker ventured to take a recording machine or camera into the field, but in the past few decades these mechanisms have become indispensable equipment for almost all ethnographers. As photographic equipment has become more portable, more flexible, adaptable to a variety of research situations, easier to protect from extreme climatic conditions, and — in simpler forms, at least — easier to afford, increasing numbers of anthropologists have made increasing use of photography in the field. Many of them develop their own film as well. A few innovative projects have recruited members of the society being studied as the photographers, thereby gaining valuable insights into how people view and represent their own society and culture.

The camera "sees" differently than does the human eye. When our photographs are printed, we see not only what we are culturally conditioned to see in the fraction of a second when the picture was taken, but also the totality of social interaction and material culture that was present within the scope of the camera's lens. In a photograph, myriad relationships and details may be held in timelessness for our later inspection, and for use by others. The photograph allows for a more comprehensive record than any verbal description could give, and acts as a control factor for descriptions made from visual observations.

Like other data, photographs reflect the inherent biases of the researcher. The decision as to what constitutes an important enough moment or subject to warrant a picture is influenced not only by the purposes of the research at hand, but also by the cultural conditioning of the person behind the lens. This has sometimes been demonstrated by comparing a sequence of photographs taken by a camera placed in the hands of a native informant and those of the "objective" fieldworker. As John Collier, Jr. and Malcolm Collier say in their excellent book, *Visual Anthropology: Photography as a Research Method*, learning to observe visually, to see culture in all of its complex detail, can be a challenge to the fieldworker. They suggest, as we have throughout this book, that anyone planning fieldwork accept the "challenge of observation." Practice in being observant is, obviously, of great value in field photography. So practice giving a second look at things in your everyday world, concentrating even on tiny details. Think how you would treat these details if you were looking through a camera's viewfinder. The art of seeing can play an important role in making photography more exciting for you and for those who enjoy your photographic work. One Kodak booklet suggests being a "head hunter" and learning to catch fleeting expressions.

With regard to how to begin photographing in the field and where to start, the Colliers note that we cannot assume that everyone wants his or her picture taken. In a few parts of the world, indeed, one may encounter religious rules against allowing oneself to be photographed at all. There may also be social constraints. In Mexico you can be arrested for photographing poverty. In some parts of Europe it is illegal to photograph strangers without their permission. From these few examples, it is obvious that societies vary greatly in what they consider to be subjects that are sensitive, or even so morally wrong or emotionally charged as to be outlawed altogether. The Colliers suggest that in photography, as in many other aspects of fieldwork, one should proceed from the public to the most private, from the formal to the informal, from the outside in; photographing first what the natives are most proud of.

If fieldworkers are careful not to overstep the bounds of good judgment, they may be able to start a rapid and accurate collection of data on uncontroversial subjects even before acquiring sufficiently extensive knowledge of many aspects of the cultural scene. As we have suggested, the first phases of fieldwork usually include a variety of descriptive processes. Mapping, sketching and photography can be used in connection with those operations. Aerial photography can, of course, also provide an accurate base for creating maps and for showing the relationships among cultural features, the presence or absence of natural resources, patterns of land use, and a wealth of other details about human relationships to the social and physical environment. Getting down to earth, if fieldworkers do not have access to aerial photographs, a series of pictures taken from some high spot may prove to be an important aid in constructing a map. If ethnographers are especially interested in the physical setting of fieldwork, a few hours' walk with the camera might enable them to get a complete overview of the community under study — the types of housing, markets and shops, transportation facilities, public buildings — the details of which would be impossible or extremely time-consuming to record by any other method.

With the passage of time and the establishment of trust, ethnographers can begin to take more informal or more personal photographs of individuals and their lifeways. We have previously mentioned that, like most modern ethnographers, we prefer to work with informants who are not paid directly for their help. This is partly because, as a general rule, avoiding direct payments improves the quality of the relationships that can be established. This in no way implies less sense of responsibility or indebtedness toward informants, but our "payments" over the years are now part of the whole complex that is friendship. One way in which we try to repay a portion of the hospitality and assistance given us is through the giving of photographs. One of us has consistently given every person a copy of each photograph in which he or she appears, with the exception of large group photographs. Although somewhat expensive, photographs have proven to be eagerly welcomed gifts and also a means of preserving memories of occasions shared by the ethnographer and the informants. One recently widowed mother of twelve said, "That is the only picture of their father my children will ever have." The giving of photographs might also be a very good thing for you to consider doing in conjunction with some of your work with informants for this course.

As the fieldwork proceeds, the ethnographer can begin to use a growing collection of photographs as an aid in structuring interviews without the sometimes inhibiting effects of formal questionnaires or verbal probes that might seem tiring or unnecessary to the informant. A carefully presented sequence of pictures on a subject about which the fieldworker wants information will channel the interview more or less within the subject area of interest, and will often help the informant to remember relevant information that might otherwise have been forgotten. Instead of interrogating directly, the fieldworker can join with the informant in examining photographs. Thus, the images become the object of discussion and the focus of attention, so that the informant has a greater sense of freedom than if he or she were being questioned directly. Photographs often call forth more than mere descriptions of what is represented and can serve as a valuable means for getting at the deeper aspects of the culture—the feelings, attitudes, values, emotions, and so on.

The ways photographs can be used in gathering information—and, as a bonus, gaining better rapport—may vary greatly according to circumstances. A friend of ours who conducted his research at a fishing beach and who did his own developing in the field established the custom of displaying a new set of pictures each week on the wall of the shop where most of the men congregated to eat their meals and buy their soft drinks. The weekly display evoked a great deal of interest and useful comment. The presence of the photos served to introduce the newcomers who frequently arrived at the beach to the idea that they, too, might expect to have their pictures taken, and that those already on the beach were not only allowing themselves to be photographed but seemed to have a friendly relationship with the man taking the photographs. One aspect of this study deserves some thought in connection with an important rule of thumb which the Colliers give on the basis of extensive experience. Pictures taken in the public domain can be fed back into the public domain. Pictures taken in private circumstances *should be shown only to the people in those circumstances.*

For the archaeologist or ethnographer interested in recording technology, photography has long been recognized as an invaluable research method. The ethnographer may, for example, take a series of shots showing some technological process. By showing such photographs to a craftsperson, the fieldworker can gain a better understanding of the tools, materials, and processes involved, including important steps that may have been slighted in the first photographs.

Photographs are also important in making inventories of material culture. In addition to tangible content that may be analyzed and/or counted, classified and correlated, the pictures may yield data on a less tangible level as well. Particularly, they may offer insight into the effect or meaning that all the tangible content observed might have for the people, the quality of life, and their methods of coping with the world around them.

One way in which the use of photographs has increased rapidly in the last fifty years is in the documentation of human interaction. The complexities of social events can be captured for future interpretation, comparison, and quantification. Collecting photographs to use as data on human interaction is sometimes especially rewarding when carried out in the form of "structured observations." This involves obtaining comparable images by photographing the particular type of social interaction under study as often as possible, under conditions that are as constant as possible. Margaret Mead and Gregory Bateson did pioneering studies of this type. (See particularly their *Balinese Character: A Photographic Analysis*, 1942.) For example, the series of comparison shots exploring how Balinese adults relate to children illustrates the inattentiveness of the hands of adults as they hold and nurse small children. Once comparable situations have been photographed, there are a number of levels at which the data in the photographs can be read. The first level involves the simple discovery, observation, and enumeration of individual variables as they appear in each picture. At this level one may, for example, be noting the number of people wearing shoes as opposed to those in sandals; the proportions of men, women, and children in groups assembled on various ceremonial occasions; or any phenomena that seem to warrant further study. On other levels of study, the correlation of variables that appear together in photographs might be meaningful, or measurable and quantifiable differences in variables might be examined further.

The use of photography is essential in any extensive study of nonverbal communication as a form of social interaction. Body posture, facial expression, hand gestures, and spatial relationships are all rapidly and accurately recorded in photographs for use in studies of proxemics and kinesics (the study of culturally patterned postures and gestures). The camera can preserve all the wealth of detail that would be impossible to capture with notebook and pencil alone.

Although you will not require an extensive plan for the project in this chapter, you might enjoy and profit from some of the suggestions made by Sorenson and Jablonko in their article cited in the bibliography (1975). Sorenson and Jablonko found that they increased the potential value of visual records by using a three-part sampling strategy involving "opportunistic sampling, programmed sampling, and digressive search." Opportunistic sampling is simply the freewheeling idea, "When something interesting happens, pick up the camera and shoot." By this means, of course, one documents unanticipated and poorly understood events as they occur. "Programmed sampling is filming according to a predetermined plan—deciding in advance what, where, and when to film. It is therefore based on a cognitive framework and a concept of significance. Pictures are taken according to a preconceived structure; there are pigeonholes to fill." Digressive search, for Sorenson and Jablonko, involved turning away from the obvious and traveling out beyond personal predilections and preconceived ideas of what is important to document. Each of the three strategies has advantages and disadvantages, but, together, "they begin to balance one another so as to increase the informative potential of the visual records."

About Photographic Equipment and its Use

We realize that students in a course such as this one will be likely to represent a great range of experience in photography, from the real beginner to the practiced near-professional. We also realize that many of you will be using borrowed equipment with which you are not familiar. We have, therefore, chosen to go into some detail on the technical aspects of photography in order that you may be able to refer to it from time to time while "on assignment."

As a first order of business, we would like to suggest that when you visit a camera shop to get film for your project you take the opportunity to look around at some of the available equipment and literature. As one who may be increasing your use of photographic equipment and supplies in the future, it is a good idea to begin to familiarize yourself with what a camera shop has to offer in supplies and in suggestions. If you are a beginner in photography, it might in fact be a good idea to start by asking for some specialized advice about the film you are there to buy, for the best choice will depend not only on the camera you will use, but on several other factors as well.

There has been a marked increase during the last fifteen years in locally established or travelling teams representing various photographic supply houses. The nature and extent of the services that these groups provide varies somewhat. You may find that one is available in your area and that a representative could come to your class to give a talk and consult with you.

The material that follows gives an overview of some of the basic concepts and terminology you will deal with using your camera. The technical side of picture taking is, for the most part, simple enough that it should not take you long to learn. In any case, the objective is to learn to take pictures to suit your ethnographic purposes, not to get a job as a professional photographer. Study the instructions that come with your camera and the film you are using, since both were written by experts. The film instructions are written for both simple and complex cameras (also simple and complex photographers). The bibliography at the end of this project gives some references you can consult if you want to extend your knowledge. This discussion concentrates on the operation of still cameras, since they are simpler to use and cheaper to own and operate than most movie and videotape equipment. Even if you are oriented toward moving pictures and videos, you will benefit from a solid grounding in the use of still equipment.

Essentially, a camera is nothing more than a light-tight box that holds the film and to which is attached the lens, which can project an image onto the film when the user wishes it to. Usually, a camera has controls attached to it that allow the user to aim the camera at the subject he wants to photograph, to focus the image onto the film, and to regulate the amount of light that reaches the film.

Beyond these minimal qualifications, the sky is almost literally the limit in terms of the elaboration and sophistication (and the cost!) of photographic equipment that is available or which can be created. It is easy to be dazzled by all of the gadgets that are available — or to be impressed by arguments proclaiming that only certain kinds of cameras should be considered at all — and to end up with something that is far too specialized, too costly, or otherwise unsuited to your needs.

Cameras can be generally classified on the bases of focusing system and size of film used. There are many combinations from which to choose. The cameras that are probably the most popular with anthropologists today are those with single- or twin-lens reflex focusing systems, which take 135, 120 or 220 film, respectively.

A *fixed-focus* camera usually has a viewfinder, which will give a fairly accurate idea of what the lens will take if the subject is distant (a landscape or building) or at middle distance (group shots and so forth), but becomes increasingly inaccurate the closer you approach the subject. Some can be used only in good light or with a flash, but more and more, really inexpensive fixed-focus cameras now can be used in a variety of situations, especially with new high-speed film (to be discussed later). Instructions accompanying these cameras generally tell how to use them under different conditions. On the whole, however, fixed-focus cameras are not flexible enough for many fieldwork uses.

Zone-focus cameras (where the user measures or guesses the distance to the subject and can set the lens to that distance) are intermediate between fixed-focus and rangefinder models. They are also generally inadequate for anthropological purposes.

Rangefinder (RF) cameras provide a linkage between the lens and the viewfinder so the user can tell not only what the lens is "looking at," but also when the image should be in focus on the film. Most commonly, two images of the subject are projected into the viewfinder, and the user turns the lens focusing mechanism until these two images overlap exactly, showing the image will be in focus on the film. Although generally easy to focus, RF cameras do not tell the user how much of the image on the film will be in focus (depth of field is discussed below), or whether the focusing linkage is working correctly. One problem with RF cameras is the "parallax error" that results from the difference in position of the viewfinder and the taking lens. This causes no real difficulty with distant scenes but becomes acute in close-ups. You can correct for parallax by tipping the camera slightly in the direction of the viewfinder after you have composed the picture. Some high-quality RF cameras have devices that provide some compensation for parallax.

Reflex cameras provide for the focusing to be done through the lens. *Single-lens reflexes* (SLRs) allow the viewing, focusing, and taking all to be done through the same lens, so the user can tell quite accurately what will be in the picture, and parallax error is eliminated. A prism, which is part of this focusing system, gives most SLRs their characteristic bump in the top middle part of the body, and this prism, along with a mirror that moves during exposure, makes most SLRs bigger, more complicated mechanically, and more expensive than RF cameras. The mirror movement also makes noise during exposure, a feature that sometimes makes unobtrusive use of the camera difficult. With a few noisy cameras, it is almost impossible to take a second shot that is "candid."

Twin-lens reflex (TLR) cameras have two lenses connected, usually one above the other. The image from one lens is reflected onto ground glass (ground so as to be "frosted" and hence make the image easy to see), so that the user can tell what the lens is seeing and when the subject image is in focus, while the image from the other lens is projected onto the film when the shutter is opened. Thus, although the TLR is mechanically more rugged and simpler than either the RF or SLR cameras, it is also subject to parallax error, since the viewing lens is seeing a slightly different image than the taking lens. These cameras are generally much bulkier than either the RF or SLR cameras.

View cameras, which usually look like accordions, are the cameras with which ground-glass focusing is most commonly associated. The lens is attached to the front of the camera body, and the position of the front is moved back and forth (and sometimes up and down) until the image is in focus on the ground glass at the back. This image, although upside down and reversed, can be studied to see what will be in the final picture and what the depth of field will be. Before the exposure can be made, a sheet of film is placed where the ground glass was. View cameras generally take large film sizes, and hence are bulky, as well as slow, to use. They are seldom useful for general-purpose fieldwork, although they may be good choices for detailed pictures at one locus, such as an archaeological dig.

Film can be classified in different ways. The kind of camera you have determines the size and types of films you can use.

The smallest commonly available roll film is about 16 mm. in width, or approximately the same width as 110 size film, which comes only in special "drop in" cartridges. The major drawback to these film sizes is that the small negatives they give (and hence any dust, dirt, or defects in or on them) must be enlarged many times to reach normal print sizes. In addition, the cartridges are inherently wasteful because they cannot be reloaded, nor can cameras made for them be used with other film types. (Note that 110, 126, 120, and 220 are manufacturers' designations for particular film sizes, though the numbers have no necessary connection to the physical size of the film.)

Drop-in loading cartridges in the 126 size have some of the same disadvantages as the 110 size; but the negatives are usually 28 mm. square and do require less enlarging to cover normal print sizes.

One of the most widely used film sizes is 135, which is 35 mm. wide. The film is usually packed in standardized cassettes, some of which can be reloaded with film by the user, who can then buy film in long rolls and make considerable savings in film costs by "rolling his own." The standard 35 mm. negative size is 24 x 36 mm., though some "half frame" cameras that use the same film make negatives only 18 x 24 mm. Since money can be saved by reloading cassettes, and since it is possible to get up to 36 exposures per roll on film that yields negatives of a fairly useful size, 35 mm. film is relatively economical. The advantage of being able to take 36 exposures without reloading can be appreciated readily by anyone who has ever been cheated of wonderful opportunities for photographs by running out of film at crucial moments. Another advantage is that this is a widely available size.

Film in the 120 and 220 sizes is slightly over 2 1/2 inches in width, with 220 rolls longer than 120. These sizes give 2 1/4 x 2 1/4-inch (6 x 6 cm.) or 2 1/4 x 2 3/4-inch (6 x 7 cm.) negatives. Generally speaking, since larger negatives yield better-quality photographs, this size of film is inherently capable of higher quality than 35 mm.

Most Polaroid films come in rolls. They do not produce negatives as other cameras do, but rather produce completed prints developed immediately after the exposure. Polaroid films and equipment are discussed in more detail later in this project.

The choice of a general-purpose camera usually involves a compromise between the physical size and weight of the camera which determines how easy it will be to carry, and the film size which determines the quality of the pictures. For most anthropological purposes, cameras giving 24 x 36 mm. negatives on 35 mm. film, or 2 1/4-inch square or larger negatives on 120 or 220 film represent the best compromise. The discussion above gives you an idea of some of the other options available. You should think through your requirements carefully before you get a camera, since "what everybody else is using" may not be suitable for you.

Many new specialized types of cameras have come on the market, including those with film discs and even talking cameras. When we first heard about talking cameras, we hoped they might be programmed to tell us things like, "You forgot to put the film in, friend," or "Listen, if you'll remove the lens cover, I'll take the picture." Thus far, however, they are limited to a few things like, "Too dark—use flash" or "Check distance." Minolta has provided its "Talker" with an on-off switch, so if you don't like your camera talking back you can shut its "mouth," which might be best much of the time when you are doing fieldwork!

Lenses are generally thought of in terms of their focal lengths and their maximum apertures or "speeds." The *focal length* indicates the approximate length of the lens in terms of the optics involved, and is important because the longer the focal length the greater the magnification of any image on the film. (Lenses with great focal length are often called telephoto lenses.) Conversely, the shorter the focal length is, the larger the field of view and, hence, the number of subjects that will be included (the extreme being the wide-angle lens). Most cameras come with lenses that are called "normal," or "standard" which means that the focal length determines that the image produced on the film will be approximately equal to the field of view of the human eye. Some lenses are permanently fixed to the body of the camera, while others can be detached and interchanged with those of other focal lengths.

Now that we have talked about camera types and lenses, we can consider the remaining two of the three basic camera controls. The first, focusing, has already been covered. These last two are directly related to giving the correct *exposure*, or amount of light, to the film, and their operation is interrelated. Generally speaking, the more light a lens can transmit, the "faster" it is said to be or the greater "speed" it has. One way, then, to control the amount of light is to vary the length of time that the film is exposed to the light entering the camera. This is done by controlling the *shutter speed*, or the speed of the mechanism that opens and closes the lens opening. At the same time, in order to ensure that exactly the right amount of light gets to the film, another mechanism is needed. This regulation is done by an iris diaphragm, which works on the same principle as the human eye, whereby the diaphragm is closed down (or "stopped down") so that the lens opening, or *aperture*, through which light enters, is made smaller or larger depending on the conditions and effect desired.

The shutter speed is usually expressed in fractions of a second. The usual progression is: 1, 1/2, 1/4, 1/8, 1/15, 1/30, 1/60, 1/125, 1/250, 1/500, 1/1000, although other speeds are of course possible, and some cameras do not go as high as 1/1000th second. (Note that these are often written on the camera as whole numbers — 1, 2, 4, 8, 15, 30, 60, 500, 1000.) Each speed is double the next slower one, and one-half the next faster one.

Beyond regulating the light, the shutter speed is important in preventing blurred pictures. An overall blur of everything in the photograph can come about if the shutter speed is slow and the camera is moved during exposure. If you have difficulties with such overall blurring, try leaning on something stable; resting the camera on a wall, a chairback, or a table; increasing the firmness of your control of the camera by holding one or both elbows tightly against your body; or, as one of us has, form a life-long habit of holding your breath when you snap the shutter! In dim light, when a particularly slow shutter speed is required, you may need to mount the camera on a tripod. In addition, you might use a cable release which operates the shutter from the end of a flexible cable so as not to jiggle the camera during exposure. A moving subject can be blurred when it is moving fast enough that it moves while the shutter is open. The faster the shutter speed (the less time it is open), the faster the motion that can be "frozen" by the camera. As one Kodak "Here's How" booklet suggests, capturing speed is best done *with* speed — a speedy film (to be discussed), a fast shutter speed, speedy reflexes, and panning. Panning is the technique of following the motion of the subject with the camera. Panning will result in sharp reproduction of the subject you are following while blurring the background.

In order to regulate the aperture, lenses are calibrated in *f-stops* that indicate relatively how much light is being let through at a given setting. The f-stops form a standard sequence (1, 1.4, 2, 2.8, 4, 5.6, 8, 11, 16, etc.), with each larger number indicating that the diaphragm has decreased by one-half the size of the opening indicated by the number just below it (i.e., f2 is half the size of f1.4). Thus, the progression is complementary to that of shutter speed.

In addition to controlling light transmission, the aperture setting controls the *depth of field*. This simply means the distance in front of and behind the principal subject in which the other objects in the picture are in sharp focus. Although you usually focus on one subject, you are interested in knowing how many other objects will also be in focus in the final picture. The smaller the aperture (the higher the f-stop number), the greater will be the depth of field. You must, therefore, set the aperture to include in the depth of field all the objects you want to record clearly. If you want to emphasize some object over others, one way is to have a shallow depth of field that covers only the principal object and leaves the others blurred.

Shutter speed and aperture together determine the amount of light that reaches the film. For example, if you have determined that f5.6 at 1/125 is the correct exposure for the scene you want to photograph, yet you want to get more depth of field by stopping down one f-stop to f8, you must then slow the shutter speed down one setting, to 1/60 in order to allow sufficient light to enter. Thus f4 at 1/250, f5.6 at 1/125, and f8 at 1/60, are equivalent exposures in that they all expose the film to the same amount of light, but they are not equivalent in their implications for depth of field or ability to stop action. You need to decide which combination of exposure settings is best for your purposes.

Film, which we have already discussed in terms of size, is basically a light-sensitive chemical emulsion coated on some kind of clear backing that is physically strong enough to take handling. It must always be kept in complete darkness until exposed within the camera to the correct amount of light. After exposure, it is processed in various chemicals that "develop" the image so that it can be seen with the eye, and then "fixed" so that the image will not fade away.

Films can be classified, in addition to physical size, on the basis of how they reproduce colors. Black-and-white films reproduce colors as shades of gray, while color films approximate the colors of the original subject. In addition, films can be classified on the basis of the degree of their sensitivity to light. "Fast" films require relatively less light to make an image, and hence are more useful for picture taking under dim light conditions. Slow films, on the other hand, require a lot of light for acceptable exposure and are more useful when photographing under bright light conditions. Film sensitivity is given a numerical rating, called *ASA* ratings in the United States and *DIN* ratings in Europe. The two sets of ratings are equivalent, although the numbers are different. In general, the faster the film, the "grainier" it looks and the less its ability to record fine detail, so there is little to be gained from using film that is faster than necessary for the light conditions under which it is to be used.

With *negative* films, the film image is the reverse of the original scene — where the scene was bright, the negative is dark, and where the scene was dark, the film was less exposed and is light or may even have no noticeable image at all. In other words, the negative is darkened where it is exposed to more light. Negatives are usually intermediate steps in the production of the final image, for light is projected through the negative onto light-sensitive paper (a photographic emulsion coated on a paper base instead of a film base) so that the result (the negative of a negative) comes out a positive in the final "projection print," usually just called a "print."

With most *Polaroid* films, there is no negative but only a finished print or transparency, and copies can be made only by photographing the print; thus Polaroid is intermediate between negative films and reversal films, which are discussed below. The lack of a negative (and, hence, of easy reproducibility), the high cost per picture, and the bulkiness of the camera make Polaroid equipment relatively unsuited for general-purpose anthropological photography. Some people, however, like to use them in addition to other cameras because the prints can be given to picture subjects immediately.

With *reversal* films, the piece of film that was exposed in the camera is processed to come out as a positive. That is, it can be viewed directly without the need for further manipulation (although the resulting transparency — so called because it is transparent to light — is often projected for easier viewing, especially if it is of small size, as is the case with 35 mm. slides). Color reversal film, by and large, has less tolerance for exposure errors (less "latitude") than negative film, and, if prints are desired, negatives must be made by a special technique. As with the Polaroid print, if the original is lost or damaged, there is no way to get another without retaking the picture.

The fact that prints and transparencies have to be displayed in different ways should be kept in mind when film choices are made. To some extent, transparencies can be made into prints, and negatives used to make transparencies, although this may raise the cost and diminish the quality of the final product. A useful way to catalog negatives is to place them directly on a sheet of photographic paper and expose the paper to light to make a contact print, which can then be studied without damaging the negatives by handling and without the expense of enlarging every negative. After the sheet has been studied, the best or most useful negatives can be chosen for enlargement, and the contact sheet kept as a record of that roll of film.

Many of the operations mentioned above in relation to developing film, making prints, and so forth, can be done by those who have access to a photographic darkroom. It might be helpful for you to practice with developing and printing if you get a chance, since it deepens your grasp of how photography works. However, for the purpose of the assignments to be given as a part of this project, it will not be necessary for you to do your own darkroom work.

Light meters, or exposure meters, are devices used to measure the amount of light coming from or going to the subject. Most of these meters transfer the light reading to a set of dials that indicate the range of f-stops and shutter speeds that will give correct exposure. Light meters can be mounted inside a camera, outside of it, or held in the hand. If the light meters are inside, they are connected to the exposure controls so that the camera can make correct exposures automatically. One must be sure to take the meter reading from the principal subject. If, for instance, you want to take a picture of someone standing in shadow but with bright sunlight behind, most meters (those which are "averaging" meters) give a reading based on the whole scene and would indicate an exposure that would result in your principal subject's being badly underexposed. It is better to over- or underexpose the less important portions of a picture and concentrate on the best treatment for the thing you want most to capture. In the absence of a meter, the literature that comes with the film usually has the manufacturer's suggested exposures for different common lighting situations.

In terms of your assignments and later use of photography, the most important thing about your photographic equipment is that you know how to use it. This comes about through practice and the thoughtful study of the results of your picture taking. *Never* take untried and untested equipment into the field or on a major assignment. As we have discussed here, you do not need to spend a lot of money on a camera. What you do want is equipment that is suited to your needs and flexible enough to be adapted to your requirements. If you do not have a suitable camera at present, consider buying good used equipment rather than cheap new equipment. Remember not to be dazzled into buying something unless its technical features will be useful to you. It is also often possible to borrow or rent supplementary equipment.

Although it is important to know, and to know how to use, the capacities of a more flexible camera, other factors are of great importance in the final results. An otherwise excellent photo may, for instance, suffer from poor composition. You may be concentrating on the principal subject and not be aware of other things in the picture that the camera will faithfully record, such as background trees appearing to grow out of the subject's head. A distant figure may seem clear to you but turn out as a small blot in the final picture. In general, good composition calls for a balanced picture, with attention being drawn to a strong center of interest. If that main center of interest is smack in the middle of the picture, it tends to look static and uninteresting; so does a picture that the horizon exactly bisects. Lines should lead into, not out of, the picture, guiding the eye to the main subject. The rectangular format of a 35 mm. camera is a useful aid in arriving at pleasing composition. Use the long axis for strongly vertical subjects by turning the camera sideways. The background can make or break a picture. It can help to set the mood, but it can also distract terribly if it is cluttered. In good weather, try shooting from a low angle to include sky. In scenic shots, it is often a good idea to include people in the foreground — but people who are looking at the scene, not woodenly at the camera. A final hint concerning composition that is often given — and often needed — is to move in close to your subject until you have eliminated everything that does not add to your picture. Some people look through the viewfinder and start backing away. This is neither the best way to compose, nor the best way to survive to take more pictures.

When shooting color film, it is generally a good idea to try to include variation in color; with black and white, try for contrast. But neither of these suggestions, nor any of those about composition above, are to be taken as rules. You may, for instance, want to portray the total greenness of a rainforest, or the total grayness of a foggy winter morning. A camera is only as good as the photographer behind it. But some people who have little technical expertise have an excellent feel for attaining good composition, for seizing precisely the right moments to catch people being themselves, and for generally capturing the spirit of a people and their ways of life on film. Such people can succeed very well as ethnographic photographers.

The Project

In past editions of this book we have simply requested that each student take one photograph in each of nine categories. Our aim was to give each person at least a variety of experience in photography. We are keenly aware that some students are involved with folklore and may want to photograph pottery and quilts, others do some archaeological work and want to photograph a range of types of artifacts, still others want to photograph human interaction, and so on. If this book was designed just for field photography, we might do well to heed the advice of a colleague and ask you to take a roll of film for each category. We are, therefore, outlining nine suggested types of photographs as before. We now add, however, that instructors and students may wish to reach agreements concerning what are reasonable and useful assignments, given the students' individual needs, backgrounds, and interests.

This *suggested* project consists of nine photographs. While only one photograph of each of nine types is required, those of you who would like to experiment more with your equipment may wish to make several exposures of various types that you can analyze for what they can tell you about your camera and its use under various conditions. If you shoot color transparencies, make sure there will be some way to project them for comparison with others in class — or you may want to have prints made from the transparencies. As you put together the photos for the project, ask yourself to what extent each could stand on its own without a caption.

For the purposes of this project (and, of course, for what you can learn from the information), please keep a record for each exposure of when it was made, the equipment (camera and lens, if you have a choice of more than one of either), shutter speed, f-stop, the film and the exposure index for it, and, if possible, the light-meter readings taken. With experience, you may not need to keep all of these records; but they are invaluable at first. Dating is the one type of record that must never be omitted.

The Photographs

1. *A home interior.* Photograph the inside of a room to show the furniture and other artifacts, and their arrangement. Such photographs are often used by anthropologists for general illustrative purposes, as well as part of inventories of material culture. If you have any supplementary equipment, such as a tripod, a cable release, additional lighting devices or flash, you may wish to use them for this assignment, although the use of available light is, of course, permissible. Correct camera settings for use with a flash unit can be determined with the aid of the instruction sheet provided with each roll of film. Select an angle of view that shows the room and its contents clearly, and a depth of field to cover everything you want in the final picture. If you use flash, aim at an angle to any reflecting surface so as not to have a reflected ball of light in your picture. A "reflecting surface" can, by the way, be used creatively in some instances, especially mirrors which can show parts of a room into which your camera cannot peek or give different dimensions to your photograph. Flash may be useful for a picture such as this, whereas it often is not when photographing people or public events because it draws so much attention to the photographer and makes activity less spontaneous. Please take as your special challenge the idea that, as an *anthropological* photographer, you want to reveal how the home reflects the people who live in it.

2. *A street scene.* Select a lively street scene, preferably one block in a shopping neighborhood with many small shops. Record something of the organization, functions, and human mix of the block. Be sure you have adequate depth of field to record the feeling and action of a whole block.

3. *Small group interaction.* Select an outdoor group activity, and make your photograph one that attempts to capture interaction, as well as the context in which the people are acting (that is, the buildings, artifacts, and so forth, that give additional clues to the nature of the group and what they are doing). You want the practice of capturing human interaction in a still picture, which means that you need to compose the picture with enough depth of field at a fast enough shutter speed, and to capture a peak moment in the interaction. Select for this assignment the exposure that best shows context and interaction, so that the resulting picture shows what the group of people is doing collectively, in contrast to a set of unrelated actions. This is an assignment for which it would be especially useful to take a few

pictures, rather than just one, so that you can learn to anticipate behavior, catch it on film, and make a story sequence.

4 and 5. *Portraits.* Next take one portrait of a child and one of an adult, preferably so as to emphasize not only the face of the person but also the context within which he or she lives, works, or plays — the playroom or play area for the child, the home or office for the adult. Again, you will want to experiment with lighting, either natural, artificial, or both. Part of the challenge will consist of putting the subject at ease so the pictures will be natural. Often this can be accomplished, at least in part, by giving him or her something to do. In working with a child, it is often a good idea to phrase your purpose in terms of wanting to photograph a doll or some other toy, so that the child just thinks of himself as helping to get the toy's picture. Perhaps you might arrange a "birthday party" for a doll or bear and invite the child to take part. Compose the portraits carefully enough to leave out objects and lights that would distract from the purpose of the picture. Remember that the camera is literal and records what you point it at, unlike the human eye, which can ignore what it does not want to see. Your major challenge is to convey the character of each person as best you can.

6. *A building.* View a building that interests you at several times of day (photographing, of course, if you like), observing from the same position, preferably north or south of the building. Note the effect of light in modeling the building and emphasizing its three-dimensional nature. Tilt your camera up, and note that the building's walls appear to be converging. Choose the exposure that best shows the building's three-dimensional character.

7 and 8. *Artifacts.* Take separate exposures of a small artifact (manufactured object) sized 3 inches or less, and of a larger artifact between 6 inches and 6 feet in size. Try exploring different angles for viewing the artifacts and different lighting arrangements. You will need at least one strong light to bring out the form and texture of the artifacts, as well as other (perhaps less strong) lights to keep the shadows from being underexposed and hence too dark for the film to record detail. Note that at close focusing distances your camera's lens has very little depth of field and you will need to stop it down as far as possible to get the artifacts in focus. You may need a tripod and cable release to help you because of the slow shutter speed, and may want to check on possible parallax error. If you have trouble in gauging distance from your lens, especially if your camera requires you to "guesstimate," and since

exact focusing becomes especially necessary in close-ups, you may want to tie a string at the front of your camera near the lens. Put a knot in the string at a distance from the camera that corresponds to the distance setting you use for the photograph and hold the string out from the camera until it touches the artifact and the string is taut. You can then drop the string and take photos at the desired distance. Use the two pictures that best show the artifacts for these parts of the project.

9. *Stop action.* Choose a lively activity, such as a sporting event with lots of quick action, and photograph the action in accordance with our earlier suggestions — use a fast shutter speed and pan with the action to "freeze" the principal subject. Concentrate on catching a peak action moment. This is another assignment for which it would be especially useful to take a few pictures, rather than just one.

Selected Annotated Bibliography

Bateson, Gregory and Margaret Mead. *Balinese Character: A Photographic Analysis, Special Publications of the New York Academy of Sciences,* Vol. 2. 1942. New York: The New York Academy of Sciences. A classic example of the use of photography in culture and personality studies. One of the few published examples of the consistent application of photography as a primary means of gathering data.

Byers, Paul. "Still Photography in Systematic Recording and Analysis of Behavioral Data." *Human Organization,* 1964, 23:78-84. Contains a good discussion of the difference between what the camera "sees" and what the human eye "sees." It emphasizes using the camera as a means of recording significant aspects of social interaction, rather than just taking pictures for illustration purposes.

Collier, John, Jr. and Malcolm Collier. *Visual Anthropology: Photography as a Research Method,* rev. ed., 1986. Albuquerque: University of New Mexico Press. This book is the basic reference for the student interested in using photography in fieldwork. It contains a complete discussion of the uses of photography in fieldwork, including the planning and executing of research that uses photography as a primary source of data.

Feininger, Andreas. *Basic Color Photography,* 1972. New York: Amphoto. A clear and concise guide to the selection and use of camera and film, applicable to black-and-white, as well as color, photography.

Mead, Margaret and Ken Heyman. *Family,* 1965. New York: Macmillan. An anthropologist and photographer combine to create an amply illustrated book about the family in cross-cultural perspective.

Rudisill, Richard. *Mirror Image,* 1971. Albuquerque: University of New Mexico Press. A story of the early beginnings of photography.

Sorenson, E. Richard and Allison Jablonko. "Research Filming of Naturally Occurring Phenomena: Basic Strategies." In P.E. Hockings, ed., *Principles of Visual Anthropology*, 1975. Hawthorne, NY: Mouton.

Steichen, Edward, comp. *The Family of Man*, 1955. New York: New York Museum of Modern Art. The great photographic collection of 503 photos from 68 countries. It has been revised and republished in several formats.

Worth, Sol and John Adair. *Through Navaho Eyes*, 1973. Bloomington: Indiana University Press. A report on some of the first innovative experiments in which members of the society being investigated were asked to make films, choosing their own subject matter.

Additional Resources Related to Photography

Directories and buying guides to photographic equipment are usually put out once a year or so by the editors of photographic magazines, such as *Modern Photography* and *Popular Photography*, and are useful summaries of the kinds of equipment available. Current issues of photographic magazines often have articles on different aspects of photography suitable for beginners and advanced amateurs.

Eastman Kodak Company (Rochester, New York 14651) supplies information on how to use its camera and film products as well as data books, "Here's How" books, and other publications on numerous aspects of photography. Most photographic dealers carry many of these publications and can get others for you, from this and other companies. Some Kodak booklets are less than one dollar, and there is a special large, inexpensive packet for the amateur.

Editors of Time-Life Books have a series in the Life Library of Photography, including ones on the camera, light and film, the print, color, etc. These books include information on the history of photography as well as current practices, are lavishly illustrated with diagrams and photographs, and are reasonably priced.

The newsletters of the Society for the Anthropology of Visual Communication (formerly Program in Ethnographic Film) are a valuable source of information about the current opinions as to how films may be used in anthropology. Also included are reviews and discussions of the ethnographic films which are currently being produced.

Project Fourteen

Planning a Community Study

I n this book we have used the word "community" loosely to refer to whatever group was chosen as the focus for your projects (for example, the church congregation of the participant observation chapter, the ethnic group from whom your examples of folklore were collected, and so forth). We have applied the term to very different types of human groupings, both formal and informal, cohesive and dispersed.

A very important branch of field anthropology, however, has been devoted to a more precise definition of the concept of community, and to the use of the community as the basis of ethnographic research. Because this "community study school" has been so influential in contemporary anthropology (and sociology), and because it has attempted to bring into a unified framework so many of the approaches discussed in this book, we feel it appropriate to round off our survey of ways to collect data in the field with a discussion of the community study.

According to one dictionary, a community is "a body of people having common organizations or interests, or living in the same place under the same laws and regulations." As such, social scientists have always studied "communities" insofar as they were interested in human groups. The terms "society" and "culture" were developed in order to discuss these groups on a higher level of abstraction; but people were actually working with communities, the collections of people whom one could observe, live among, and describe. A more formal usage of the community concept developed early in this century, primarily among sociologists interested in studying the city as a "natural laboratory of social science" (Hollingshead 1948, p. 136). At that time, the city was defined in terms of its *norms*, and sociologists were frequently interested in improving the lot of those unfortunates who, for one reason or another, were unable to live up to those standards. In this rather restricted use of the concept of community, the unit of study was not simply everybody living in the same place at the same time, but only those who conformed to certain patterns of approved behavior.

In the 1920s, a group of sociologists at the University of Chicago turned away from this normative (and interventionist) approach to the community. They saw the city not as a natural laboratory in which they could practice social engineering but as a unit of *analysis*. According to the members of the "Chicago School," the role of the social scientist was to study particular communities in terms of their history, development, population, and organization. Their goal, then, was not to work to see that everyone conformed to normative standards, but to observe and account for variation as it naturally existed.

The most frequently cited achievement of this group was the study of "Middletown" by Robert and Helen Lynd, published in 1929. This was the first truly analytical study of a "typical" American town; although the Lynds were trained as sociologists, they made use of some of the basic techniques of the early ethnographers. They studied the ordinary, day-to-day lives of the people with whom they lived on a protracted basis, and, from that "inside" view, they were able to analyze the institutions, organizations, and other aspects of the social structure of the town. The Middletown project thus brought the notion of "interaction" into the vocabulary of community study. The point was not to define standards and then try to fit everyone into them, but to see who actually did what, with what, to whom, and with whom. The community, then, need not be localized. As long as people interacted in a regular way with each other, there might be said to be a community structure—even if they communicated only by mail or telephone.

One of the most prominent anthropologists at the University of Chicago at that time was Robert Redfield, who was very much influenced by the sociological group. As a result, he was able to combine his training in ethnography with the concerns of the community-oriented sociologists. Redfield was in turn influential in shifting some of anthropology's attention from tribal societies to more modern societies, via the organizing principle of the community study.

Redfield's definitions of community are no longer fully accepted by anthropologists, but they are of sufficient historical importance to deserve discussion in some detail here. Redfield was concerned with what he termed the "little community," which he felt was the most characteristic form of human settlement throughout history, and even in the modern world. When researchers first enter any community, they will see only a mass of confusing activity—a totality that almost engulfs them because it cannot yet be fully comprehended. Using the ethnographic approach, the researchers begin to study the parts that make up this whole and then proceed to discern how the parts fit together. When the analysis is finished, the totality can once again be seen. This time, however, it makes more sense because they know how it is constructed. The "little community," for Redfield, is the basic unit of observation for analyzing how people put themselves and their productions into some sort of meaningful order.

Redfield (1973, p. 4) defined the "little community" in terms of four major dimensions:

- distinctiveness (the group itself must be conscious of the fact that it is a group; outsiders must also recognize that the group is a group)
- size (the group must be small enough to allow members to interact with each other on an ongoing basis)
- homogeneity (members of the group must share a set of institutions, attitudes, values, etc.)
- self-sufficiency (the group must not be dependent on another group, for such dependence would affect the distinctive character of its own institutions)

These criteria are based on a model of the community derived from traditional anthropological research in tribal societies, and it has struck some critics as unfortunate that Redfield chose to treat the community even in modern societies as if it were as homogeneous and self-sufficient as a hunting/gathering band. In fairness to Redfield, it should be pointed out that he did not view the "little community," wherever in the world it happened to be, as if it were a totally detached entity, complete unto itself. Rather, such communities were seen as parts of a continuum of complexity that ranged from the "folk" to the "urban" society. While it is impossible to set precise boundaries and say that one thing is a "pure" folk community, for example, it is certainly clear that some communities more nearly approach one end of the spectrum than another in terms of their organizations and institutions. Since its contacts with the "great tradition" surrounding it will be minimal, a group that is relatively more "folk" can then be treated as if it were a self-sufficient unit—but *for purposes of analysis only.* Using such a definition, Redfield was able to study the Mayan village of Chan Kom in Mexico as a social entity whose institutions, activities, values, and so on could be analyzed in the same way as those of an isolated tribe, even though it had a marginal relationship to the sophisticated, literate cultural tradition of Hispanic America.

Redfield's work stimulated an interest in "peasant" studies—analyses of traditional communities within the urban civilizations of North and South America, Europe, and Asia. Although it is not necessary to survey this vast literature for the purposes of this chapter, at least one group of studies should be singled out because of the importance of the theory of community study that grew out of them. These are the studies of rural Irish life by Arensberg and Kimball. For various reasons, Arensberg and Kimball were unable to view the Irish village as a completely self-contained unit, as Redfield had done with Chan Kom; but they nevertheless recognized the importance of community as an organizational feature in all types of societies—the more urbanized ones as well as the "folk" type.

In the 1950s and 1960s, Arensberg and Kimball were concerned with defining the notion of the community for analytical purposes, and with setting forth certain principles for studying a community in the field. Their first and most basic premise was that a community is not a "thing" but a *process* (Arensberg and Kimball 1965, p. 1). It is, therefore, incorrect to ask, "What *is* a community?" Rather, one should ask, "What does a community *do*?" As a result, the researcher is advised to ". . . seek those regularities in the relationships among individuals that are revealed in their activities with each other and with the physical items in their environment" (1965, p. 2). Whereas the social psychologist, for example, would study such regularities of interaction by setting up a controlled experimental group in a laboratory setting, the anthropologist (or sociologist) can use the community as a "living laboratory"—not as a field for working out social welfare plans, but as a setting for the formulation and testing of hypotheses.

What, then, in the view of Arensberg and Kimball, does the community do that makes it appropriate for the testing of hypotheses about society and culture in general? First and foremost, "Communities seem to be basic units of organization and transmission within a society and its culture" (Arensberg 1961, p. 248). Thus, once again we have the criterion of community as defined by communication and interaction, but with one important difference. It is not enough simply to communicate any old thing—

one must communicate *culture*. To refer to a somewhat more psychological frame of reference (which Arensberg and Kimball do not explicitly do), the community is the agency of socialization and enculturation, the vehicle by which children or newcomers are taught their statuses and roles as members of a sociocultural system. (See the discussion in project 12.) In this way, Redfield's criterion of self-sufficiency can be retained; although the community may be in almost constant contact with communities elsewhere, perhaps to trade goods and services, each community may very well retain its own autonomy as long as it retains its most basic institutions of socialization. (Depending on the particular group, these institutions may include the family, the legal system, or religious organizations.) A collection of such interconnected but autonomous communities may, indeed, form a cohesive "society," although such composites may better be described as "plural societies," rather than as homogeneous "folk" societies.

Because the community, wherever it is and whatever its particular features may be, is a unit for the transmission of culture, it may be studied not only as a thing of interest in and of itself (as Redfield studied Chan Kom), but as a microcosm of the sociocultural system in which it is embedded. The true nature of the community study, then, is *naturalistic* (that is, observing the group as it is, rather than as a part of an experimental design), and *comparative* (studying communities as representatives of cultures that can be compared with one another, rather than as independent units studied separately).

One studies a community, then, in much the same way that one studies a tribal society in classic ethnography: in totality. Although one may enter the field with a specific hypothesis to test, or a particular area of culture in which one is most interested, it will always be necessary to do as complete a study as possible in order to understand the contexts in which the more specific behaviors occur. It is impossible to study everything, but the goal of the community study is not "exhaustion in detail," but "depth in view" (Arensberg and Kimball 1965, p. 32), which is achieved by a "multifactorial" approach (p. 31). In other words, it is important not to use just one of the research tools that have been outlined in this book—one uses all of them, if at all possible, and perhaps invents new ones that seem especially appropriate in the particular community under study. The depth interview, participant observation, genealogical survey, life history collection, analysis of personal documents and of folklore, and all the rest are part of the complete community study; not because they could ever possibly provide every last fact and figure about the place, but because they shed light on so many different facets of the same behaviors.

The study of a town in the United States by Barker and his associates is a conspicuous example of a community study in which "exhaustion in detail" was, in fact, chosen over "depth of view." This research team used a systematic method of observing and coding behaviors, specifically interpersonal interactions, making thousands of minute notations of everything that happened in specific localities. Barker, however, is a psychologist primarily interested in patterns of interaction, not an anthropologist interested in the sociocultural context of those interactions. While Barker's method is interesting and deserving of attention by anthropologists embarking on a community study, it should be noted that his study would not represent a "complete" community study as Arensberg and Kimball have defined the term.

One of the most important modifications within anthropology of the Arensberg and Kimball approach is that pioneered by Julian Steward. He rejected the premise that a community can be studied as if it were fully representative of a wider social system. In order to understand that sociocultural system, he said, it is necessary to study all the different types of communities that make it up, as no one of them is likely to be fully representative. This is an even more complex job than the "complete" study of just one community, and so Steward favored the use of a large research team, preferably one representing various other social sciences as well as anthropology. Smaller groups within this main research team would each be responsible for studying in depth one of several selected communities. The most important thing about doing such research is to ensure *comparability* — to make sure that everyone is asking the same questions, in the same ways, observing the same types of things. Each community must be studied and compared in terms of: its *local units* (households, streets, neighborhoods), *special groups* (races, castes, classes, ethnic segments), and *formal institutions* (political parties, church groups, service clubs).

The most impressive example of Steward's approach to the community study is the massive Puerto Rico project that he directed in the 1950s. The aim of this project was to study the social anthropology of Puerto Rico. Although the island is a distinct society with characteristic forms that make it different from other societies within the broad Hispanic American tradition, there are many varieties within it. What are the roots of these variations within Puerto Rican society, and how are the various communities integrated into the whole of the Puerto Rican sociocultural system? In Steward's theory, the different types of Puerto Rican communities were based in large part on ecological adaptations. Communities in the mountains, for example, would clearly be different from those on the seacoast, from the point of view of adapting and obtaining a subsistence, and this difference would affect their respective social structures as well. Despite these ecological variations, however, all would bear the distinctive Puerto Rican stamp, marking them all as members of the same overall society. Therefore, a number of different communities representative of the various types of ecological adaptation found on the island were selected, and each was studied ethnographically using research methods that had been standardized for use by all members of the research team. They all relied on:

- interviews, both random and directed
- collections of case histories
- participant observation
- key informant interviewing (interviewing specialists)
- use of archives, records, and other written documents, both historical and contemporary
- standardized questionnaires

In a more narrowly bounded study, Raymond T. Smith analyzed three communities in Guyana in order to compare varieties in kinship and domestic organization. Smith's problem was that although there is something that might vaguely be termed a "West Indian kinship structure," and while there may well be a typically Guyanese version thereof, it is useless to speak in such generalized terms when the variations actually reach down to the local community level. By selecting three communities that had different subsistence bases, and by studying the domestic arrangements in these groups, he was able to get a somewhat clearer view of what Guyanese kinship really means. A similar study was undertaken by Edith Clarke in Jamaica.

The Project

Although you will not have the time or the resources to carry out a full-scale community study, you are now in a position, after having carried out some of the individual projects in this book, to make some tentative plans for a more comprehensive undertaking.

Your project, then, is to write a *proposal* for a community study of your own home town or neighborhood, or any other community with which you are very familiar. You may write it either as if you were planning to do it yourself, or as if you were answering questions from another anthropologist who wanted to do it and was seeking your advice as an expert on this community.

Remember that a community is any *group* based on regular associations among persons, but it may be either a compact settlement with well-defined boundaries or a dispersed group whose boundaries overlap with those of other communities. William Pilcher's study of longshoremen in the city of Portland is an example of the latter (1972). Although the people in question do not live in a spatially defined community, they form a community because they share various important interactions, values, and attitudes with each other, many of which they do not share with others in the city.

You may refer to the rather extensive outline prepared by Arensberg and Kimball (1965, pp. 36-40) that details the means of collecting data in a full-scale community study, or you may restrict yourself to the following more general outline.

I. Delimiting the community for study
   A. What are the boundaries of this community?
      1. Geographic boundaries (e.g., rivers, mountains)
      2. Demographic boundaries (e.g., the community ends along a religious or linguistic border — in the community people speak Italian and attend a Roman Catholic church, while across the street people speak Greek and attend an Orthodox church)
      3. Official boundaries (e.g., governmentally sanctioned town or township lines)
   B. What specific factors make this community different from others in the same vicinity?
   C. What factors link the community to others in the same vicinity?
   D. What are the facilities for getting to and around in this community?
      1. Transportation
      2. Communications
II. Entering the community
   A. Are special arrangements needed to enter the community?
      1. Permission of the local sheriff's office or chief of police
      2. Cooperation of village elders
      3. Passports and visas

  B. What is the best way of getting to the community (fastest and least expensive)?

  C. Is there some time of year when it is better to arrive than any other? If so, why?

  D. What special clothing or other equipment will be needed for living here for an extended period? If special clothing or equipment is necessary, should the fieldworker bring it along, or is it cheaper and/or more readily available in the community itself?

III. Establishing the researcher in the community

  A. Who should the first contacts be?

   1. Officials

   2. Social leaders

   3. Others

  B. If you think it would make a difference to contact one or the other of these people immediately, explain why.

  C. Is there anyone to avoid initially? If so, explain why.

   1. Groups

   2. Individuals

  D. Where should residence be established?

   1. Buy own home?

   2. Rent home, apartment, or room?

   3. Board in someone's house?

    a. With a single person or family?

    b. With what kind of people?

  E. How should the research project be explained?

  F. Should the researcher seek work in the community (other than the research per se)?

   1. If so, why and what kind? If not, why not?

   2. Should the researcher join, or attend meetings of, local organizations (churches, clubs, etc.)?

  G. Should the researcher, if single, date local people? If so, why? If not, why not?

  H. If the community is large and has many people living in it, who would be the best informants? Why? How should they be chosen? How should the researcher cultivate the friendship and cooperation of informants? Should informants be given a regular salary? Periodic gifts? Or would such remuneration be considered inappropriate? If something needs to be given, what is the best thing to give (money, food, favors)?

IV. Methodology (Assuming that the researcher has no one specific area of culture that needs to be studied more intensively than any other)
  A. Discuss in some detail the data-gathering techniques you would use to gain "depth in view" coverage of the community. You may use those discussed in this book, or devise ones you think would be more appropriate to the local situation.
    1. Are certain techniques more appropriate to use for certain people than for others? If so, why?
    2. Are certain techniques more appropriate to use for collecting certain types of data than others? If so, why?

(In answering these questions, be very specific about how the research is to be carried out. Do not simply say, "Study attitudes by means of a questionnaire." Say a few words about what types of questions to ask, when to survey, whom to survey, and how and when to pretest.)

  B. Are there any situations in which using a camera or a tape recorder would be considered either offensive or otherwise inappropriate? If so, why? How would you compensate?
  C. In describing your research techniques, be sure to include some notion of what kinds of equipment are necessary (camera, film, tapes, measuring devices, etc.). Also address the question of data recording: how should field notes be kept and stored? How is it best to organize them for efficient retrieval?

V. Leaving the community
  A. Should the researcher report officially to anyone about departure plans?
  B. Should going-away presents be given to one's informants? Should presents from informants be expected? If so, what is the polite response to such generosity? (That is, will the researcher be expected to reciprocate even after leaving the field?)

VI. The post-field period
  A. How should the researcher organize the analysis and writing up of data?
  B. Presuming it is advisable for the community to be aware of the project, should the researcher seek local approval

before having it published? If so, who should be asked? How?

C. Once it has been published, how should the report be disseminated to members of the community? How many copies? To whom?

D. Add any other comments about the conduct of the study that you think are particularly appropriate to the situation in your community.

If you like, you may do this project as a group effort. Suppose that you were approached to plan a Steward-type study of aspects of United States culture. Several people in the class could then discuss the study of their own communities in the larger context of "United States culture" (or a regional subculture, if you prefer). In this case, you would have to be very careful about standardizing your methodology sections so that the studies would be comparable. You could also do a study like that of Smith or Clarke on a specific topic: the comparative study of family organizations in selected communities in the United States.

Selected Annotated Bibliography

Arensberg, Conrad M. *The Irish Countryman*, 1988 (original 1937). Prospect Heights, IL: Waveland Press. The revised version of a classic community study.

Arensberg, Conrad M. "The Community Study Method." *American Journal of Sociology*, 1954, 60:109-124. A concise summary of some of the methodological and theoretical points raised in this chapter.

Arensberg, Conrad M. "American Communities." *American Anthropologist*, 1955, 57:1143-1162. An application of the community study method to a classification of types of contemporary United States communities.

Arensberg, Conrad M. "The Community as Object and as Sample." *American Anthropologist*, 1961, 63:241-264. Sets forth the major theoretical premises of the approach.

Arensberg, Conrad M. and Solon T. Kimball. *Culture and Community*, 1965. San Diego: Harcourt, Brace and World. A compendium of various theoretical, methodological, and descriptive articles written by these two pioneering researchers.

Arensberg, Conrad M. and Solon T. Kimball. *Family and Community in Ireland*, 1972. Gloucester, MA: P. Smith. A reprint of a classic study.

Barker, Roger G. *Ecological Psychology*, 1968. Stanford, CA: Stanford University Press. A detailed survey of the theory and method involved in the study of interpersonal interaction within a community framework.

Bell, Colin and Howard Newby. *Community Studies*, 1982. London: Allen and Unwin. An excellent review of theory and method, with detailed reports on some major community study projects; especially useful for its inclusion of studies by European scholars, which are generally less well known to students in the United States than those done by researchers based in North America.

Clarke, Edith. *My Mother Who Fathered Me*, 1966. London: Allen and Unwin. A comparative study of three Jamaican communities and their kinship organizations.

Cohen, Anthony P. *The Symbolic Construction of Community*, 1985. London: Tavistock. A brilliant exposition of the prevailing contemporary theories of community and the methodology of the community study.

Hollingshead, August B. "Community Research Development and Present Conditions." *American Sociological Review*, 1948, 13:136-146. A concise history of the sociological tradition of community studies.

Kimball, Solon T. and William L. Partridge. *The Craft of Community Study: Fieldwork Dialogues*, 1979. Gainesville: University Presses of Florida. Letters exchanged between a professor and student in the course of a field project in community study; an insightful glimpse into the learning process.

Lynd, Robert S. and Helen M. Lynd. *Middletown: A Study in Contemporary American Culture*, 1929. San Diego: Harcourt, Brace. The classic study of a United States community.

Pilcher, William W. *The Portland Longshoremen: A Dispersed Urban Community*, 1972. New York: Holt, Rinehart and Winston. A readable account of a contemporary United States community, noteworthy for its focus on a group defined by common interest rather than by geographic proximity.

Redfield, Robert and Alfonso Villa Rojas. *Chan Kom: A Maya Village*, 1990 (original 1934). Prospect Heights, IL: Waveland Press. One of the pioneering efforts in the anthropological version of the community study approach.

Smith, Michael G. "Community Organization in Rural Jamaica." In Michael G. Smith, ed., *The Plural Society in the British West Indies*, 1965. Berkeley: University of California Press. Although the examples in this volume are Caribbean, the book is an important contribution to both the theory and the method of community studies, particularly in the pluralistic societies of the modern world.

Smith, Raymond T. *The Negro Family in British Guiana*, 1956. London: Routledge and Kegan Paul. An analysis of three communities, comparing variations in kinship and domestic organization.

Steward, Julian. *Area Research: Theory and Practice*, 1950. New York: Social Science Research Council, Bulletin 63. Contains a good section on community studies, as well as a thorough summary of the theoretical and methodological considerations underlying the Puerto Rico project.

Steward, Julian, et al. *The People of Puerto Rico*, 1956. Champaign: University of Illinois Press. The massive ethnographic end-product of the community study research undertaken by Steward and his colleagues.

Index

191